UNDERSTANDING
PRAYER

*An exploration of the nature,
disciplines, and growth of the
spiritual life*

Edgar N. Jackson

SCM PRESS LTD

334 01718 1

First published in Britain 1980
by SCM Press Ltd
58 Bloomsbury Street, London WC1

Typeset in the United States of America
and printed in Great Britain by
Richard Clay Ltd (The Chaucer Press)
Bungay, Suffolk

Understanding Prayer

*Also by Edgar N. Jackson
and published by SCM Press*

The Many Faces of Grief
Understanding Loneliness

TO MY PARTNERS IN PRAYER

CONTENTS

❦

PART ONE

A Setting for the Study of Prayer

1. PRAYER: MAN'S BASIC LANGUAGE

DEEP within the soul of each person is an ever unsatisfied need and desire to communicate. We become the persons we are by this intricate fabric of human relationships that we call learning, experiencing, being. Yet deeper than the words we speak and hear is a yearning for something more than words can ever satisfy, when deep speaks unto deep, and the wonder of being is amplified by the fullness of meaning.

We break through the captivity that makes each man an island by the languages we speak. Yet each language is itself an achievement of learning and a discipline of acquired meanings. If you have ever been stranded in a land where your language did not communicate, you know the feeling of relief experienced when you met a stranger of kindred tongue.

I remember such an experience some years ago when I visited the city of Patras on the Gulf of Corinth. The Greek I knew was "classical." The Greek the inhabitants spoke was a modern variation as different as Latin is from Italian. I walked the streets in lonely silence for hours. There were questions and comments I could have shared, but I was very much alone. Finally I wandered into a small factory where artisans were making copper kitchen utensils. I asked the price of an item, and was greeted with a torrent of unknown words. My blank look showed my ignorance. Then one of the workers, identifying me as an American, went to the door and called in a loud voice. A few seconds later a man arrived and said, "I used to live in Brooklyn. Now I am retired and live here.

What can I do for you?" Yes, he could talk with me, and for me. The floodgates opened to permit communication. A small crowd soon gathered to listen, enjoy the humor, and to share in the political and philosophical insights that were freely exchanged. The change in situation came about, not because we were different persons, but because the channels of communication had been opened. Someone had been found who knew the language, who could translate.

Something similar happens when we learn the language of prayer. We wander through life filled with unanswered questions, and comments we would make if there were anyone to listen. Often in our loneliness we find no one concerned about the deeper meanings of life. The language we use in speaking with others carries only a part of the communication our beings would make. We struggle to learn a deeper language that can satisfy the yearnings of our being to know even as also we are known. Many persons go through life with their efforts to learn this language of the soul thwarted because there is no one to teach them the basic language of the soul, prayer.

Sometimes the institution that should know most about prayer misdirects those who turn to it for guidance. The church often leaves its people with the impression that prayer is primarily a matter of pious word formulations. The minister will rise before his congregation and announce, "Let us pray." When the "Amen" is voiced, it is assumed that the praying is over. Actually, those in the congregation experienced a liturgical act, a formal part of worship, which might have no more bearing on true prayer than reciting a creed may have on faith and conduct.

At other times a common practice keeps us from getting a full view of the wonder and meaning of prayer. As children, we heard our mothers say to us, "Come now, brush your teeth, say your prayers, and get in bed." It is understandable that many adults conceive of prayer as a routine act most appropriate to childhood.

This restrictive concept of prayer as a limited and partial practice keeps us from discovering its full meaning. The New Testament speaks of man's need to pray continually. We are asked to use the whole of our being at all times, that we may discover the deepest values within ourselves, the fabric of human relationships that sustains us in living, and the meaning of that cosmic otherness that relates us to the world of nature and supernature.

Professor Maslow of Brandeis University speaks of a self-fulfilling principle that makes it possible for a person to find the full health of his nature, to grow into the full stature of his being. This could well be a definition of what takes place in true prayer. In it a person uses the energy of his mind to direct the movement of his living toward the finest goals he can create.

This concept of prayer offers greater opportunities than are possible through the formal repetition of set words. Prayer at this new level engages one's whole being in a quest for the richest and fullest possibilities of living. Such prayer is not easy, inasmuch as it requires strenuous self-discipline. It is the focal point toward which the energy of life is directed in the effort to become spiritually mature.

Those who would learn this fine art of prayer must desire it more than anything else in life. They must firmly believe that by finding the true meaning of prayer all other meanings will be enhanced. Faith so directed and acted upon brings forth fruit.

This prayer is a language embracing more than words, for words are the tools of the mind. The disciplined life of prayer uses the combined resources of body, mind, and spirit to realize the possibilities of living that grow from the creative union of the best use of body, mind, and spirit in integrated living.

When the disciples observed Jesus and the unusual qualities of his life they sought to understand how it happened. They were quick to realize that it was not in his formal education, his acquired skills as a teacher or preacher, but rather that the unusual powers let loose within him were the achievement of his mastery of the discipline of prayer. So they said to him quite simply, "Master, teach us to pray."

Jesus started with his disciples where they were, using the language they knew and the familiar illustrations from their daily life. From there he stretched their minds and spirits by his teaching and his example until they had found the power within themselves that made it possible for them to turn the world upside down. But until they put behind them all small attitudes of mind and old modes of thinking, they were unable to put to use their desire to find the full meaning of prayer.

It is not easy to learn a language. A child uses the listening and trial-and-error method to learn the mother tongue. A student uses intensive study and practice plus his experience with his mother tongue to learn a foreign language. How much more difficult it is to learn the language of the spirit, where feelings are more important than words, and aspirations more significant than syntax. The total person then seeks to find the basis of communication that lifts his whole being to the highest level of achievement. In his new experience of relationship to God he uses listening, imagination, self-discipline, and creative intuition to produce the finest fruits of prayerful living.

2. TO PRAY OR NOT TO PRAY

❧❦❧

THE person who sets out to find the full meaning of the life of prayer in our day will encounter obstacles unknown to previous generations. Students of human history will point out the early roots of prayer and testify that it is a hangover from man's ancient need to placate the unknown forces of nature. Students of human personality will examine emotional needs and say of prayer that is is a counterpart of the magical thinking that believes it can control the outer world merely by wishing. The physical scientist defines the structure of matter so precisely that there seems to be little place for the processes of prayer to influence it. The astronomer pushes the frontiers of the universe farther and farther out so that the Creator seems more remote and so less interested in the complaints or aspirations of the swarming creatures on a cosmic speck, the Earth. Those with sociological interests say that the benefits attributed to intercessory prayer can be explained merely by the knowledge of group support. The experts in personality function, the psychiatrists, find alternate means for integrating the resources of the individual so that prayer becomes for them unnecessary. How, then, is the serious student of prayer to reply to these points of view so widely held in our generation?

The student of prayer would willingly admit that these observations are true enough from the scientist's base of operation, but that they have little or no relevance at the point of meaning. The scientist describes; but the philosopher, the mystic, or the religious thinker defines. The scientist records and classifies; the man of prayer deals with meanings. His point of reference is himself, his own life and his meaning for it. He does not deny any truth that science discovers, but his search is for a larger truth that is beyond the realm of science and the scientific method. Man is the measure of his science for it is his mind that is the creator of it. The man of prayer is more concerned with the man who is a scientist than he is with the limited product of his scientific imagination. If this product gets in the way of man's understanding of himself, he is not afraid to challenge it.

There are three points where this challenge must be made for the sake of the scientist who questions the validity of prayer and for the general community which desperately needs to find adequate meaning for life itself.

First, PRAYER IS INTENSELY PERSONAL. Just as a person can breathe for himself alone, so the process of prayer is a personal communion and communication. Science on the other hand by its very nature tends to be impersonal. It is concerned with the accumulation, correlation, and analysis of data. Anything as essentially personal as prayer appears to be out of place in a world that has geared itself to theoretical and applied science. But the man of prayer is not anti-scientific. Rather he is concerned with something of great personal importance that is beyond the scope of ordinary scientific interest.

Jesus emphasizes the private nature of prayer. It was his practice to retire quietly by himself to engage his whole being in the discipline of prayer. This he did early in the morning before others awoke. He spoke on occasion of praying unobserved in a closet, a place set apart. He admonished his followers to "Pray to the Father in secret" and also in secret to find the answers that come through this personal communication. He ridiculed those exhibitionists who prayed in public places to demonstrate their piety. He commended those who dared honestly to look into their own nature. He gave no indication that he separated those qualified to pray from those who were not, but rather urged all men to find the relationship within themselves that made the approach to God's kingdom possible for them. In a culture where the value of the intensely personal is not recognized, it is inevitable that any process as bound up with the depths of being as prayer is should have to struggle for acceptance.

Second, PRAYER IS INTERNAL, NOT EXTERNAL. Our age has distinguished itself by technical mastery of the external. We have been so preoccupied with externals that we have neglected the inner being who gives meaning to all the rest. It is difficult for us to imagine how great is our captivity to a world of science. My father, born in 1877, saw the advent of the electric light, the telephone, the internal combustion engine, the automobile, the airplane, radio, television, atomic and nuclear power, space flight, and electronic computers. The technological development within his lifetime has been more rapid and spectacular than in the total span of history preceding his day. It is easy to explain why man has concentrated on these achievements rather than that quiet and unspectacular quest for inner meaning.

The newcomer to the study of prayer soon learns that it is impelled from within rather than prescribed from without. Thus, prayer moves against the main current of our intellectual and scientific interest. Its realm is an uncharted no man's land which exists within each individual as he explores the hidden meanings of his own life. "When you pray, use not vain repetitions" is the warning against the formulary or rote concept of prayer. The admonition, "I will pray with the spirit and with understanding also," sets the course of this soul exercise toward sincerity of exploration and genuineness of understanding. The heart of the preparation involves a person's spirit and a quest for understanding. By such control, the mind reverses the trend of our technological day, and seeks inner fulfillment rather than outer manipulation. Yet, this mood of prayer is not in competition with the world of technology. Rather it is essential to the wise use of its achievements.

Third, PRAYER IS A SPIRITUAL DISCIPLINE. Our age is highly disciplined in the matter of things, powers, and resources. A three-year-old child knows more of mechanical resources and the discipline required to use them than Saint Francis ever knew. But Saint Francis knew the world of nature and himself with quite a different kind of knowledge. Our discipline and skills in manipulating external things have been developed at the expense of the inner discipline essential to true prayer.

The scriptures speak of prayer as a primary concern of life. "Men ought always to pray," "Give yourselves continually to prayer," "Pray without ceasing," and "The effectual fervent prayer of a righteous man availeth much" are examples of the centrality of prayer in New Testament life. This then is a quest for a discipline quite different from what most of us know. We are well aware of the signs and symbols that direct and control the flow of traffic. Yet the highway of God is traveled with reckless abandon.

This prayer we speak is a main-line concern. It is personal, intense, internal, and an achievement of strenuous self-discipline. By its very nature it moves against the major preoccupations of our day, and while it is not in open conflict with this cultural mood, it must struggle for its being against the inroads upon attention that are the inevitable part of our pattern of life.

The question then is not "To pray or not to pray?" as much as it is "How do I pray in a world like this?" The critique of science upon the life of the spirit is invalid because it is irrelevant. The impact of a scientific era upon the quest for spiritual meaning in life is powerful just because it is diverting. Those who would find the meaning of their spiritual natures through the discipline of prayer can do it, but they will have to work harder to succeed because the external world clamors so noisily against the small voice of the spirit.

3. PRAYER AND SCIENCE

WHILE science raises questions about some aspects of prayer, it tends to clarify others. While technology directs man's attention outward, the theoretical scientist lives in a stratosphere of contemplation that creates a climate of mind friendly to prayer. Lest we assume that science is antagonistic to the spirit of prayer, let us examine what science can do to throw light on the creative processes of consciousness that we call prayer.

We are so close to the conflict between nineteenth-century science and the science of the twentieth century that we cannot easily see how basically different the two centuries are. The nineteenth century was interested in taking things apart to understand how they work, and then to make them work for man. It was a century of mastery and control of the external world. The practical fruits of nineteenth-century science have occupied us in the twentieth century, even though something of profound importance was taking place quietly behind the scenes in the studies of the theoreticians. Now, two-thirds of the way through the twentieth century we are in the enigmatic position of acting largely on the basis of the science of the last century while we are seeking to find the meaning for life of the science of our own century.

The top theoretical scientists of Europe and America have moved well beyond a materialistic science with its implicit materialistic philosophy of life. Harrison Salisbury reports after interviews with top Russian scientists that although the Soviet philosophy is based on the dialectical materialism of the last century there are now no atheists among Russia's leading men of science. The mood of this century asks searching questions about the nature of man and his spiritual life and it is not satisfied with quick and easy answers. For science itself has asked big questions about matter, space, and infinity and it has no simple and easy answers to offer. Dr. George Russell Harrison, Dean of the School of Science at the Massachusetts Institute of Technology, says that the universe appears to be more like a great thought than like a great thing.[1]

Modern science spends much time and energy trying to understand, weigh, and measure some things it has never seen and probably never will be able to see, for if instruments sensitive enough were developed, what it would be looking for would not be there. Ultimate reality appears to be made up of qualities, energies, and motion more nearly spiritual in nature than the traditional ideas we have had of the material. Science, therefore, investigates phenomena with unseen and eternal properties, and this is what a person does in prayer.

Modern science has found that formerly used definitions and modes of measurement are no longer adequate. The speeds are too fast, the distances too great, the pressures too intense, and the powers too tremendous to be put into the old words without breaking the words away from the meaning they once

[1] *The Role of Science in Our Modern World* (original title, *What Man May Be*) (New York: William Morrow and Company, Inc., 1961).

had and setting them adrift in oceans of meaning they cannot encompass. The astronomer coins new words to communicate with fellow astronomers, the biochemist develops his vocabulary appropriate to biochemistry. The astronaut has his own jargon and the physicist knows what he is talking about when he talks with another physicist. But the uninitiated, listening in, would consider it as a tower of Babel. Some of the specialized language has been domesticated. We hear words like light-years and megatons without flinching. But the simple truth is that science has led the way in developing new languages for identifying things that cannot be seen or heard. This is not unlike the activity of a praying man who translates into the language of the spirit his need to communicate in ways that are well beyond the capacities of old words and old moods. So he has good scientific and religious precedent for building a form of communication that satisfies his soul.

The twentieth-century scientist works from the premise that there is an underlying unity in creation. This faith that no future discovery can ever deny the truth of creation, but will rather fulfill it, provides the research principle for a unified field theory. It verifies the scientist's faith in order, pattern, and design running all through creation, the known and the unknown. This faith differs in focus but not in nature from that of the praying man who believes that there is divine meaning and purpose in all that is, and that through disciplined consciousness he can increase his knowledge of it. Brought up to date it is the same basic feeling the Psalmist expressed when he said, "The earth is the Lord's and the fullness thereof, the world and they that dwell therein."

The questing minds of our century are aware as never before of the mystery of creation, but unlike the typical detective story, the more one knows the greater the mystery becomes. Yet the scientist makes a great leap of faith when he assumes that his mind is an adequate piece of equipment for instituting and pursuing the quest for truth. He knows that there have been errors in the past that have been corrected with time. He knows that scientific judgment has on occasion been faulty, but he also believes that underlying the inadequacy of the individual consciousness there is a cumulative process of science that is self-correcting and with time and patience will unfold more and more of the nature of creation. Unless the scientist had such faith in his own mind he would find neither the incentive nor the direction for his labors.

The questing mind of the man at prayer assumes a similar faith in the capacity of his spirit to respond to the spiritual truth that can be revealed as the result of his searching and seeking. He knows that there have been errors in the past and that well-meaning persons have given assent to ideas and practices that could not survive the test of time and spiritual maturity. But he also has faith in the sensitivity of his spirit to respond to spiritual truth. Thus he continues his search like the scientist who seeks to learn more about his world. When the world of nature is revealed to be more wonderful than he imagined, he reorganizes his theories about the new wonder revealed. The man of prayer appropriates the truths of science, the insights about the nature of man, and uses these as guides to the development of his spiritual nature. This is an act of faith, perhaps the most daring act of faith the human is capable of, for he assumes in this quest that there is something within him that is akin to the creative power that pervades nature. Because of the special quality of self-consciousness, man is not content to rest his judgment solely on rationalization. He knows of the inner capacity for response that goes beyond the structures of logic. So, as then the scientist likens the universe to a great thought, he pays tribute to the power of his own mind. The spiritually sensitive individual, aware of the stirrings of his spiritual nature, is no different from the scientist when he likens his universe to a great prayer.

The scientific mood of but a few decades ago was one of condescension or even antagonism to the practice of prayer. Science today accepts the possibilities of prayer as a valuable discipline of life, and accords validity to the basic assumptions about man, nature, and life that motivate those who pray. The restricted views of man and the universe in nineteenth-century thought have yielded completely to the twentieth century with its expanding view of man and his universe. Science now provides validity and support for the spiritual quest, and joins in the search for the spiritual controls and creative discipline that can make it safe for modern man to live with the products of his scientific achievement.

4. A SPIRITUAL LIFE IN A SPIRITUAL UNIVERSE

LAST evening I sat for a long while on the brow of a Vermont hill thinking about this chapter. The wind whispered gently in a grove of pines behind me. A full moon rising in the east dimly outlined the White Mountains. A solitary light in a farmhouse in the valley below showed that its tenant was still about. The bark of a dog resounded from another direction and penetrated the silence of the night with friendliness. Overhead the Milky Way stretched itself from the northern horizon to the south as far as the eye could see. We are a part of that galaxy and yet it seemed separated and far off. A jet bomber from the nearby airbase streaked across the sky, adding its running lights to the Milky Way and seeming more nearly a part of it than I did in my thoughtful observance. The light in the valley went out, leaving only the moon to flood the landscape with its light. I realized once again how feeble man's incandescent lamps are compared with the moon. The bomber with its pinpoint of light dotting the sky streamed out of sight, leaving the Milky Way uncluttered by man as it had been for untold billions of years. In solitude I pondered how little man and his knowledge, his science, his efforts at control really touch the infinite and timeless works of God. We delude only ourselves if we think we are the masters of creation. We find ourselves only when we have the courage to face the reality of a creation that reaches out endlessly in space and time in all directions. In this we find our bearings not by the claims of knowledge that is so puny, but through faith that unites us with a wonder-filled creation that can be known only in part by humans. What a tragedy for faith when our limited minds become limiting minds. What a source of inspiration and wonder when our limited mental resources are used to swing wide the doors of faith, so that our souls may see. The great potential of our natures is our ability to be faith-filled, spiritually endowed beings.

Man's quest for knowledge and control at the sacrifice of wisdom and love has alienated him from the relationship that could sustain his spirit. The New Testament speaks of God in terms of spiritual quality, the evidences of creative energy that are primary and indivisible. God is light, power, truth, spirit, and love. These are not so much words that define a quality as they are clues to a quality that is indefinable. Man cannot know the full nature of God because man's knowledge is finite. Yet, such limitations do not prevent man from standing in awe and wonder before the creative energy of the universe, thankful that his consciousness can make him aware of a little and his faith can sustain him in his belief that the little is the clue to the whole.

What do we mean when we speak of a spiritual universe? Simply this: that the only answers adequate to meet the deep emotional and spiritual needs of man must, of necessity, be spiritual. The yachtsman who launches his craft in Maine does it secure in the knowledge that the principles of sailing and navigation are everywhere essentially the same. If he builds his boat to obey the laws of the sea in one hemisphere he can travel secure in the knowledge that the laws of the sea will be the same in the other. The laws of nature and the orderliness of the universe give security to man's quest for spiritual meaning. His aspirations are not stranded in a universe unconcerned. At every point the truth he discovers is infinitely valid, and if it is not he knows he must extend his search to find the essential truth rather than deceptive appearances. The built-in qualities of his consciousness verify the nature of that of which he is conscious. Just as the lungs are meaningless without air, and the eyes without light, so man's spiritual consciousness is meaningless without the objective reality which verifies its nature, its right to exist. When man launches his barque of faith he does it with the knowledge that faith is not a disease or a foreign element in creation, but is rather the product of the special endowment that makes him what he is, and is continually verifying that nature.

What then do we mean by a spiritual life? The spiritual life is the process of perpetual reality-testing that goes on when the spiritually endowed creature works to realize the full meaning and benefit of his endowment. It is the process of producing the faith that is essential to the validation of life itself. At first this may resemble the act of pulling one's self up by one's bootstraps. In one sense this is inevitably so, for the self must use the self to fulfill the self, but this is not as strange as it at first seems.

Where does the scientist generate the faith he needs to carry on his research? The practice of faith produces the faith that verifies the practice. This has always been the case. The artist has faith in his ability to paint a picture before he lays his brush to canvas, but he must act on his faith in order to verify it. The builder has faith in his materials and his design before he begins construction, but until he acts on his faith he has no way of verifying it.

The process of achieving great meaning for life is an extension of the practice of faith. Man believes in the value and meaning of his existence. He lives by his principles and thereby verifies them. Jesus understood the condition of the diseased, outcast, and despairing. Yet, his eyes focused on what they could become. He believed so intensely that his faith was contagious, and the diseased were made whole, the outcast were accepted, and the despairing found new faith. We know how fear can be communicated and how contagious anxiety can be. It is equally true that the creative emotions can project themselves in fruitful relationships. The spiritual life is one that believes in its value so much that it acts on its belief and in so doing establishes the validity of its premise. It is an experience that cannot be denied by another although others may fail to achieve it. The man born blind cannot deny the reality of the seeing man's vision, though he himself has not experienced it. The spiritual life is at work to establish personally the evidences of spiritual purpose revealed throughout the cosmic order. If there is plan, pattern, and order everywhere else, I want to be a part of it.

This then provides the mood and atmosphere within which the serious student of prayer approaches his subject. He sees the possibilities in the spiritual view of the universe and the psychocentric nature of man. He knows the practical and theoretical importance of faith as a creative ingredient in life. Through prayer he seeks to bring these three elements into a productive working relationship.

It was the director of a medical research foundation, Dr. Alexis Carrel, who wrote:

> Today, lack of emphasis on the religious sense has brought the world to the edge of destruction. Our deepest source of power and perfection has been left miserably undeveloped. Prayer, the basic exercise of the spirit, must be actively practiced by men and nations. . . . True prayer is a way of life; the truest life is literally a way of prayer. Prayer is not only worship: it is also an invisible emanation of man's worshiping spirit—the most powerful form of energy that one can generate. . . . Prayer is a force as real as terrestrial gravity. . . . Properly understood, prayer is a mature activity indispensable to the fullest development of personality. Only in prayer do we achieve that complete and harmonious assembly of body, mind, and spirit which gives the frail human reed its unshakable strength. . . . When we pray we link ourselves with the inexhaustible motive power that spins the universe.[1]

This is the understanding we would have of prayer as we move on in our exploration of its nature, meaning, discipline, and fruits. So important a resource for life cannot be ignored without suffering tragic loss. So important a resource for life cannot be appropriated without dedicated effort and directed action. Prayer is the language the spiritual man develops in communicating with the sources of power manifest in a spiritual universe. In learning the language we are all beginners, but even our lisping of spiritual consciousness is so rewarding we would know more.

[1] "Prayer Is Power," *Reader's Digest* (March 1941).

PART TWO

The Process of Prayer

5. MAN: THE PRAYING CREATURE

WILLIAM JAMES, the father of American psychology, writes, "The reason we do pray is simply that we cannot help praying." Man must seek "the true, the intimate, the ultimate, the permanent me," and he does so through his communion with "God, the Absolute Mind, the Great Companion."[1]

Modern concern with the problem of "selfhood" is an effort to define that something within man which is more than the sum total of his weight and measurement, his skills and his intellect. It is an effort to find again, in the midst of our preoccupation with things material and scientific, those qualities of the human spirit that make man the distinctive creature that he is.

Prayer is the traditional instrument by which the self-conscious person realizes in personal terms the possibilities of his God-consciousness. But prayer is not merely a traditional instrument. It is also a source of power within the structure of personality. As with electricity, power comes through a point of contact. We plug into a source of energy that is provided. Only then shall we experience the benefits it can furnish. Something about man has led him in all times and in all places to try to plug in to some power beyond himself that he was aware of, and appropriate it for his own use.

If prayer is as we have said a basic language of the spirit, it must share qualities common to communication systems.

[1]*Psychology* (New York: Henry Holt, Inc., 1910), I, 316.

There must be a sender, a receiver, and a medium of exchange. We are familiar with such instruments of communication as radio and television. A transmitting station produces electronic waves that have a potential meaning which is brought to reality only through the instrumentality of a properly tuned receiver. The receiver is so designed that it transforms electric waves to wave lengths within the range of the human ear. Both the receiver and the transmitter are dependent upon a medium through which the waves (the vehicle of communication) can pass without being grounded, destroyed, or dissipated. A car radio loses its signal when it crosses a steel bridge, because at that point the waves are disturbed by outside forces. Radio Free Europe encounters communication difficulties when other transmitters seek to destroy the signals by jamming the frequencies. Signals at a distance become so faint that they are lost. These mechanical factors are so much a part of our experience that all of us know what they mean. The communications we employ in prayer may be similarly interfered with, grounded, or destroyed.

If consciousness is a form of electrical energy, as some psychologists claim, it is easy to see how the processes of consciousness may be subject to influences similar to those encountered by mechanical contrivances.

Man, the creature with highly developed consciousness, may be responsive in varying degrees to the creative consciousness that is everywhere in evidence in the cosmos. This is a part of his nature. Even though he may deny it, the statement remains true, for he lives by values. When his values are small his life is small, and when his values are great, his life shows the marks of greatness.

A man's concept of his own nature is a key factor in his outlook and activity. What he truly believes about himself affects his behavior patterns. Here we would paraphrase the famous question of the Psalmist, "What is man that thou art mindful of him," by asking, "What do I think of myself?"

When man takes a base view of human nature his actions betray his outlook. If he thinks of himself merely as a biochemical entity he reduces life to the functions of biochemistry. Thinking becomes no more than a chemical function with complicated cause-effect processes. The search for life-meaning is no more than chemical interaction according to the person with such a viewpoint.

If man is merely a social creature, then the values of his living are acquired from society. Something of this process is observed in the Soviet Union where man is seen as a socio-political being, and the other value-creating sources of life are denied. While this philosophy may help to make an efficient political institution, it thwarts something important in the nature of man himself, and in order to preserve himself man must fight against it.

Even that man who thinks himself as made in the image of God faces a hazard. His God may be too small. Man is not guiltless in the matter of image-making. Strangely enough, it shows in human behavior, i.e., the vengeful who justify their vengeance as the reproduction of the righteous act of a wrathful God.

But man cannot be explained fully by biochemistry, social necessity, or inadequate religion. There is something about his nature that totals more than the sum of his parts. This plus-factor must be taken into account before he decides on the boundary lines of his own nature.

Man is also an image creator. In the very process of thinking, he sparks off images. The words he uses have a pictorial quality. The thinking process is invaded and saturated by imagery. We can scarcely suppress the parade of imagery that bombards our minds. Images come in various sizes, shapes, and colors. We select, sort, and classify as we will, and the choice tells quite a bit about us. Moses long ago knew the life of the Jewish community was threatened by small-sized, graven images. He tried to produce an adequate image of God, the lawgiver, as an essential to preserve the lives of his people on their trek into the Promised Land.

Man is also an artist. His creative nature struggles to produce meaning and beauty. No explanation of his nature is satisfactory that does not take into account this demand for creativity at the core of his being.

Man is also an explorer. His curiosity is a growing edge on his knowledge which keeps him continually reaching out into the unknown. Without some explanation of this quality of man we do not come to terms with his nature.

Man is both an introvert and extrovert. He looks deep within his being to try to understand his nature, and also he looks out upon the universe around him to try to understand his place in it.

Man is also a spiritual being. None of the small views of man and his nature can account for the unusual qualities of his consciousness. If we would understand man, the praying creature, we would have to move far beyond the mechanical, the social, and the biochemical to acquaint ourselves with the image-maker, the artist, the explorer, and the spiritually endowed being, for all of these qualities have to be taken into account when we consider the praying creature. For the highly evolved spirit, prayer is an effort to create the most challenging images, produce the most artistic interpretations of life, explore the inner and outer frontiers of being, and come to terms with the endowment of spirituality which is both the burden and wealth of mankind.

Perhaps there is no more sublime object in all creation than a man at prayer, for here the effort is made to lift self-consciousness to its highest plane. Here man seeks to bring together in their highest possible form of integration the four qualities C. G. Jung defines as the essence of being: sensation, thinking, feeling, and intuition. Without any one of these essential qualities, man, the praying creature, is incomplete. With all of them brought together in sensitivity and discipline, man achieves a transcendent quality in his being. Then he is mindful of himself as something more than self. He creates the supreme image, the God image, and seeks to pattern his life on it.

6. HOW PRAYER DEVELOPS

As in the rest of life, prayer has its developmental aspects. Growth is experienced in mental and spiritual processes as well as in the physical. An understanding of this growth process is essential to our understanding of the nature and variations of prayer. Since prayer is highly individual, it shares the infinite variations that accompany growth.

The growth process is influenced by heredity, the heritage of the past; and by environment, the physical, social, intellectual, and spiritual climate of life experience. A third factor is the dynamic quality of interaction always at work between the individual and his environment which affects growth. A fourth condition, difficult to define, is perpetually at work modifying life. It might be called the something other, the spiritual sensitivity, the revelation, the intrusion of an outer consciousness upon man's self-consciousness.

Heredity endows us with a natural inclination for prayer. The sensitivities peculiar to man have been in the process of development for hundreds of thousands of years. The human brain shows the marks of transitional slow growth from the instinctual toward the rational. As with the telltale evidence of the growth rings of a tree, the whole life history of man on the earth is found in the development of the brain. So some of our actions are still more subject to intuitive responses than to reasoned action. A racial inheritance, as Jung calls it, is part of the standard operating equipment of every human begin. Some of the archetypes, the deeply rooted hereditary traits, show the remnants of sensitivities that were once important but are now unused. Like some of our physical equipment—muscles in the ears, hair on the body, and the vermiform appendix—our brains show the marks of equipment once significant for life but now only of vestigial importance. Telepathic sensitivity once important now appears to have been outmoded by language communication. Intuitive action has been limited in many respects by reasoned action. Yet the remnants of the past are there, and some of these remnants are rudimentary sensitivities that can again be brought into a higher state of activity by discipline and practice.

Archeological, anthropological, and psychological studies all point to some endowment in man that leads the individual beyond himself. In the presence of danger it may be activated, as with soldiers who in combat are stirred to prayer. In disciplined action it can become a developed sensitivity. It is a resource that cannot be ignored when we think of man's basic equipment for prayer.

The environment is an important contributive element in the process of prayer. A culture such as India that glorifies the holy man would be more conducive to the life of prayer than a culture that elevates the rational as in our Western scientific culture. Many of the values taught by a culture are subtle and indirect. What is valuable in one culture may be unimportant in another. Sometimes the emphasis is on the superficial and trivial. When emphasis is on external status, the values are tinged by the external. When emphasis is on the internal, quite different ideas as to what is valuable ensue. The Eskimo with his training in cooperation is fulfilling a collective need for security in a hazardous climate. He cannot understand the reasons for competition which have been so emphasized in our economy.

The teaching of rote prayers often anesthetizes our spiritual sensitivities. The capacity of awe and wonder so essential to effective prayer is often stunted in children who are drilled in the form and formality rather than the feelings of genuine prayer. Growth in spiritual communication is enriched by that culture where creative and individualistic expression is permitted. Environment involves more than geography and mores. It also embraces emotional climate and spiritual atmosphere. All of these conditions tend to influence and condition the development of our attitude toward and our practice of prayer.

The dynamic quality of the individual personality is important to the development of prayer. Personal growth is a perpetual process of interaction between the endowed individual and the environment in which he develops. It is not only the answer to the question, "What happens to him?" but also to the question, "What does he do to his circumstances?" Each person undergoes recurring experiences where heredity and environment amalgamate to emerge as a new being. The result may be a Saint Francis, a John Woolman, a Saint Paul, or a Dietrich Bonhoeffer. Each individual with his unique qualities is able to find a new and personal meaning for prayer as an instrument of spiritual growth. His deep needs, his unaccountable sensitivities, his feelings expressed or repressed, are at work as a dynamic resource to modify life.

In the encounter of the individual with his world something

new is continually emerging. Illness may touch an Ignatius Loyola, the sight of human slavery an Abraham Lincoln, the strange warming of the spirit may influence a John Wesley, and from that point on life takes a new direction. Sometimes the events are small and seemingly of no consequence, but the inner being often has a delicate balance that is awaiting the sensitive touch of circumstance. Often great personal importance is given to the small events that turn the course of a life. A door of insight may be swung open by a slight breeze of circumstance to let light flood into darkness, and a spirit that has been dormant may be illuminated. The moments of illumination of the mystics verify the fact that the dynamics of the self are powerful directives of life. The something new that floods life may be of great importance to the processes of prayer as the point where the self encounters the "Beyond-Self" and is changed.

When all allowance is made for heredity, environment, and the dynamic encounter of self with the "Beyond-Self," there is still something else important at work in the process of prayer. It is the point at which the "Beyond-Self" seems to take the initiative, and intrudes upon the consciousness of man. The experience comes to man through revelation, a vision, an illumination, or an awakening. It is an experience that defies definition. The outsider remains unconvinced by the appropriate vocabulary. The insider considers the vocabulary as an inadequate vehicle to convey the meaning and experience. Interpretation is difficult since it does not fit in the area of sensory perception. Paradoxically, the spiritual design of man is activated by the spiritual quality that originated the design. Stated more simply, it is deep crying unto deep. Francis Thompson has tried to put the feeling in poetic form in "The Hound of Heaven." The initiative appears to come from outside of the individual. Even though he tries to avoid the encounter, he fails utterly for it overwhelms his consciousness.

Many of the experiences of man cannot be explained without it, though mere explanation never fully contains the dimensions of the experience. We cannot probe the depth meaning of prayer without taking serious account of this fourth element.

The end result of these four factors that contribute to the development of prayer is a quality of personal achievement where man realizes the fullest possibility of his nature. It stimulates imagination, brings to life the dormant psychic sensitivity, and brings the praying individual into contact with a meaning for life that is far beyond ordinary living. It represents a point of privileged inner growth. The circumstances for its achievement cannot be predicted or planned like some life activity. However, when it happens all the rest of life is modified by it. It becomes the pearl of great price, the right relationship with eternal things that is sought first that all else may be found through it. Life never reaches its full spiritual growth without it, yet for many it is an unrealized part of life.

7. PRAYER AND COSMOLOGY

AN important question to be considered in the process of prayer has to do with the nature of the universe. How does the universe relate to man's spiritual nature? Does the universe support man in his efforts to realize the full potential of his spiritual nature?

At different times in his religious development man has had quite varied views of the universe. Modern man in developing his prayer life cannot ignore the nature and meaning of the rest of creation.

Some persons view the universe as capricious and unpredictable. In this context man ascribes good or evil to nature according to the magic he can bring to bear on them. Actually there is no real law or order in a universe so conceived. The priests of Baal held such views. They thought they could play upon the sympathy of their deities to make it rain by gashing themselves with rocks and uttering frenzied incantations. They felt that the power of their priestly rites would have a proportionate effect on the forces that controlled natural events. To this day there are flagellants who by such self-abuse seek to control the phenomena of nature.

Those who believe in an unordered universe occasionally seek to impose their arbitrary wills on natural events. Some religious groups practice a type of *quid pro quo* in cosmic bargaining. Certain benefits are expected of God in exchange for their acts of devotion or penance. The practice of magic has meaning only in an unordered universe. The workers of magic demonstrate their control and power by manipulation. The type of prayer we have considered so far has little or no meaning to the person who views the universe as disordered, capricious, and subject to manipulation. Such a universe would be in perpetual chaos, torn between the conflicting interests of selfish men.

Other persons think of the universe only in terms of unalterable law and order. The meaning of their universe is bounded by a materialism that allows no place for man's spiritual aspirations. In such a scheme prayer has no place or meaning. The cosmic order is rigidly and unalterably set. The practice of prayer could have only psychological value, beginning and ending with the person who prays. Prayer in this context would be hard to distinguish from self-hypnosis. In this materialistic view of the universe man and his spiritual aspirations are contradictory. Prayer when viewed from this perspective is quite different from what we have been considering.

Still other persons think of the universe in purely mechanistic terms, with precise order being dictated by mechanical law. No place is accorded to purpose or meaning. Spiritual aspirations are ruled to be completely out of order and inconsistent with such a cosmology. In this kind of universe prayer is unthinkable and illusory.

In contrast to the capricious, materialistic, or mechanistic view of the universe there is the view of a spiritually-ordered creation. The cosmos is no less one of law and order, or of cause and effect. Rather a new dimension is introduced. Here man seeks to discover the meaning of a spiritual law and order to which his consciousness is attuned. Prayer is now employed as the instrument for the discovery of spiritual order. The premise is that man's spiritual nature and aspirations must find support in the cosmic order that created them. Man would then be engaged in his quest for ultimate meaning in trying to discover the spiritual laws that undergird his spiritual consciousness. This would make of prayer the instrument of discovery of a higher order at work in creation.

This is the view of the universe held by Jesus. Early in his ministry he made it quite clear that the spirit of the Lord was upon him because of his nature and deeds. This made it a personal achievement, not because of unusual circumstances or special privilege, but because he set himself to discover the spiritual meaning of existence.

In symbolic form the temptations Jesus experienced in the wilderness are a definition of his view of the nature of the cosmos. First, he was tempted to use magical power to turn stone into bread to satisfy personal need. This he refused to do, affirming that man's essential being must be satisfied by something more than bread, and that his goal in life was not to use spiritual power for selfish interest but to do God's will. Prayer, therefore, is to be used not for selfish gain, but to bring the self into accord with God's will.

In his second temptation Jesus was invited to use spiritual power to counteract the laws of the universe. In this instance the law of gravitation was to be contravened by throwing himself down from the temple in a spectacular manner. This he refused to do. It was his conviction that man's spiritual obligation was to work within the framework of natural law in his quest for spiritual law. The dramatic effect of violating the laws of nature and getting away with it must be resisted in order to find the way of using the law and order of the natural world to fulfill the higher demands of the spiritual kingdom.

In his third temptation Jesus was invited to consider the more direct and effective methods of social and political power to overcome the world. But he resisted this for he knew that the mastery of the inner kingdom was more important for his purposes than the overlordship of a temporal kingdom no matter how vast. The spiritual kingdom is the Kingdom of God, and it is achieved through inner control and self-mastery.

In other words, Jesus made it clear that there are no quick-and-easy, magical, or spectacular ways to the inner kingdom of spiritual power. This inner kingdom does not violate the law and order of the universe, but rather fulfills it by the wise use of its resources in the process of finding and making personal the resources of the spiritual order.

Throughout his ministry Jesus demonstrated his faith in the dependability of the natural order. A mustard seed that co-operates with the chemistry of the earth, the light of the sun, and the moisture of the atmosphere has all the potential required to become a large bush. Man, when he is ready and willing to cooperate with the laws of the spiritual realm, has all that is necessary to become a son of God.

Jesus was so convinced of the fact that the resources of the universe sustained the spiritual nature of man that he personalized it and called it "Father," the ultimate term for a friendly, creative relationship. But he did not think of this source of spiritual power as indulgent, for this very indulgence would have made it undependable. Rather it was concerned, loving, and willing to enter into the sufferings of man, that by so doing men might be able to grow in understanding and self-fulfillment.

In this dependable universe of natural and spiritual law and order, man has a special place. But it is not a place that guarantees him freedom from suffering and trial. Rather it is the place whereby he can discover endless meanings through all of his experience, if it is held up to the full light of spiritual possibility. Here prayer comes to its highest quality for it is the process of self-examination and spiritual seeking that keeps all experience subject to its highest possible interpretation. So a cross is a symbol of triumph, and disease is a challenge to healing power, and man is granted freedom that he may use it to know and do God's will. In this kind of a dependable universe we live and pray.

8. THE UNDISCOVERED SELF

THE process of prayer is one of self-discovery. This may seem strange at first. Most of us are of the opinion that we understand ourselves more than we do others. Yet, there are conditions of training and habit that erect barriers to self-understanding. Paul Tournier draws a distinction between the person and the personage. His viewpoint is that while we get to know ourselves as a personage the true person often remains obscured. The personage is the composite of the varied roles we play. Thus, we may be the student, the parent, the employee or the employer, the social or political entity, and the member of religious and community institutions. When we consider the amalgam of these several roles to be the real person, we deceive ourselves.

The personage is engaged in a round of activities that occupy most of his time: breadwinning, amusement, family and community responsibilities. The daily round of role-playing builds the very image of the personage. The impact of outside influences is so constant and real that the hidden inner resources remain latent.

External influences can be cruel and damaging. Childhood experiences may leave deep scars on the person. "Call a child stupid and you make him stupid." The more sensitive a person is, the more easily he is injured by the external judgments that are passed, no matter how false they are. So a beautiful girl may think she is ugly just because of the remarks of a jealous companion. A person with strong inner resources may react with timidity and fear when chiding remarks are made about him. Angers, fears, hatreds, and jealousies may overwhelm a person from without, and he may lack the self-control to regain his perspective. The suggestions of others may be so powerful that they override his own reasoned judgments.

Forces at work within us sometimes drive us to act contrary to our better judgment or to neglect to act in worthy and helpful ways. Saint Paul and Saint Augustine confessed they were troubled by these conflicts within their own personalities.

Not until this twentieth century have we discovered some of the reasons for this troublesome and unreasonable behavior.

Man's consciousness is now known to be complicated and more far-reaching than he had imagined. The work of Frederick W. H. Myers, who coined the term *subliminal consciousness*, and Sigmund Freud, who explored the subconscious and unconscious, provided us with helpful insights into motivations that extend beyond the easy range of reason.

Myers developed the idea of consciousness which resembles a spectrum. Our eyes are capable of seeing the colors of the rainbow, but we know that these are not all of the colors that exist. Fast-moving rays of light on the violet end of the spectrum are not visible to the unassisted eye, but we know of their effects. The ultraviolet waves can cause sunburn. The faster-moving rays can penetrate the body and are used for medical purposes as X-rays. The fact that we cannot see them merely means that our sensory equipment is not designed to see them. But their existence and influence can be easily verified by means that supplement our eyesight.

On the opposite end of the spectrum the slow-moving rays pass beyond our vision, but we can feel them. The infrared rays are used in physiotherapy, and slower-moving light radiation is heat-producing in varied form and degree. So on either end of the visible spectrum there is light radiation important to our existence, but beyond our vision.

Myers claims that our consciousness functions similarly. We have levels of consciousness that do not come under the control of reason and ordered judgment. At one end of the spectrum of consciousness we have the experience that is subconscious, preconscious, or unconscious. Some of it is reflected in habit patterns and behavior forms. We may even speak of some of them as characteristics. Some things in our subconscious or unconscious may trigger anger or fear. Early childhood experience before recollection is stored in this lower level of consciousness and can cause behavior that is hard to explain. A child frightened by a barking dog so early in life that the event cannot be remembered may have an acute emotional reaction when a barking dog comes near. These conditioning forces in life may have more control over behavior than our conscious and reasoned judgments. These could well have been the things about which Saint Paul and Saint Augustine were bothered.

In more recent years students of psychology have been exploring a perimeter of consciousness that might be called superliminal or superconscious. This would be the experience that moves off the other end of the spectrum of consciousness, and explains the spiritual sensitivity man is aware of. It centers on the paranormal, the psychic, and the experiences that religious persons have referred to as visions—the prophetic awareness or the seer's insight. Such experiences have an important influence on life but are above and beyond the normally recurring life experiences that are controlled by reason and calm judgment. These superconscious manifestations employ capacities of the mind not easily adapted to laboratory-controlled conditions. But, they are no less valid a part of life because of that.

We have also learned in recent years methods of approach to levels of consciousness that resist rational examination. The dream, the gesture, the patterns of speech, the free associations that surge forth when our minds are put in neutral and our speech is spontaneous, furnish clues to the ferment deep within our beings. The psychologist, psychiatrist, and psychoanalyst seek to understand and interpret the realm beyond consciousness. They have learned that it is possible to retrieve experiences to the place where they can be dealt with consciously. The process resembles our struggle to remember a name that has not been used for a long time. We have stored it in our memory bank, the subconscious, but must now strive to bring it to the surface of consciousness.

Prayer as we think of it is a valuable aid in trying to bring some of the fringe areas of consciousness to the place where we can deal with them wisely and well. Our fears, angers, and unreasonable behavior can be modified if we develop the skills of prayer as a way of opening doors into our undiscovered selves. This is not to say that prayer is merely quiet intro-spection and self-examination, but that is certainly one of its component parts.

Sometimes illness is caused by a chemical imbalance of the body resulting from emotional disturbances. These stresses can be traced to behavior or attitudes about which we feel guilt and shame. During the quiet moments of prayer the disturbing act or attitude can be brought to the surface where we can examine it carefully and calmly and adopt a wise course of action in relation to it. Having done this, the emotional state is modified and with it the body chemistry. What might be called a healing takes place because the disruptive portion of the being was restored and placed under the control of reason and right action.

Prayer may well be one of the most important resources available to man for the exploration of the frontiers of his consciousness so that they may be understood and brought under the control of the self that he would like to have always in command, his best self.

9. PRAYER AND THE MIRACULOUS

PEOPLE frequently confuse the processes of prayer with efforts to work miracles. It is important to understand the distinctive differences between prayer and the miraculous.

Just what is a miracle? The word holds different connotations for different people. It is a term we customarily use for a remarkable occurrence. A medical doctor may say, "If he gets well it will be a miracle." The patient gets well. Is this, then, a case of a miracle or is it the result of natural phenomena? We speak glibly of the miracles of the space age, of electronics, and even of miracle plays. We read of miraculous escapes from turnpike collisions or airline crashes. Quite obviously the word is used variously and loosely.

Generally speaking, the word miracle is used to identify the unknown, the unfamiliar, or the incredible event which exceeds the boundary of understanding or logical explanation.

A shower of meteorites falls from the sky and frightened people gather about referring to it as a miracle. The snow cross appears in the sky and some persons interpret it as a sign, a miraculous communication of divine import. A Spanish galleon appears off the Mexican coast and the Aztecs think it is a miraculous visitation. A helicopter descends in the wilds of the Upper Amazon and the natives think it is a miracle. Often a natural event that appeals to superstition or strong emotions of fear and uncertainty is called a miracle.

A person born in 1900 might be engaged in imaginary conversation with a person who died in 1900, and it could be assumed they were talking about two different worlds. The events surrounding the age of flight, medical advancement, electronics, and space exploration would be taken quite for granted by the person who has grown up with them, but they would be unknown, thus easily considered "miraculous," by the person who had them suddenly thrust upon a mind that was unprepared for them.

The very word "incredible" shows that it deals with a capacity to believe, to accept as credible. When something happens that a person could not believe possible, it is for him incredible, and therefore it is held to be miraculous. When a person is unable to comprehend the infinite resources of power in nature, he imputes supernatural origins to such phenomena. When Jesus employed spiritual resources to accomplish unusual events in the lives of his friends they called him a miracle worker. They made a big fuss about the things he did, but paid little attention to the reason or purpose behind him. This disturbed Jesus considerably for he disliked the image of the wonder worker. In fact, he cautioned those who were the healed not to mention what had happened.

The greater a person's capacity to believe, the narrower is his incredibility gap. Jesus was so highly disciplined in spiritual matters that his massive faith produced unparalleled results. He was using God-given resources available to all who would achieve the discipline. But those of little faith who did not believe enough in Jesus' central message of man's spirituality missed the opportunity for a mature faith by seeing only the superficial appearance which they labeled as miraculous.

Jesus carefully avoided the use of the word "miracle." When he referred to unusual acts, he spoke of them as "signs" or "mighty works." He was apparently disappointed whenever people gloried in the spectacular rather than in the spiritual resources that lay behind them. He tried to convince his hearers of the spiritual power within each of them. All too often they missed the point. Jesus emphasized again and again that there was no miracle except that of the God-endowed life. Only when life is brought under the full power of God are there unlimited power resources. The power of faith within the individual releases the resources capable of making men whole. Jesus lived by and taught this principle. Miraculous events were trivia inasmuch as all of creation was undisputed evidence of the great miracle, the nature of God in action.

Jesus sought that middle zone of activity between doubting the power of God that could be released through those who believed powerfully and the hazard of tempting God. How could man tempt God? Evidently God is so desirous of making his powers available to mankind that he accepts the risk of rejection. Free will makes possible both use and abuse. God is indeed tempted by men who request a show of divine power contradictory to his revealed purpose. Men continually petition God to act in areas of human capability where wise men can and do succeed. Much of the illness of our day and age is the direct consequence of physical and emotional abuse. The discipline of prayer could resolve many of the problems of life. These benefits come not through divine fiat, but rather by way of the wise relationships that produce the fruits of prayer. The achievement is the outcome of man's own spiritual effort, and not a miraculous intrusion of divine power into the affairs of men.

Jesus made it clear that his purpose was not to set aside laws but to fulfill them. To this end he sought to discover the spiritual dimensions of natural law. He saw the potential in humankind for the multiplication and escalation of their native endowments. Men now could rise above their natural inclinations, and become spiritual beings. In this process the natural power within could come to realization through spiritual discipline.

Jesus used prayer as the perpetual sensitizer of his being to the will and purpose and power of God. He strenuously struggled to keep his natural resources subject to his spiritual nature. He worked unceasingly at this process, and his disciples and followers knew this to be the secret of his power.

When conceived and used in such fashion, prayer is not a pious search for miracles, but is the process by which the only true miracle can result. Courageous and audacious believing is inseparably bound with creativity. Faith is the evidence of things not seen, the advance proof that what has not happened yet will happen. Jesus believed in people so effectively that his followers were captivated by his confident spirit. Jesus was convinced that there was tremendous power in the spiritual natures of men waiting to be released. We who live in an age of atomic science can understand what he meant. Long eras had passed before mankind discovered the tremendous power inside an atom of hydrogen or uranium. But it was there all the time waiting to be discovered by those who had imagination and resourcefulness enough to find it. Jesus felt that the same thing was true of the spiritual natures of men, that they were endowed by God with great power, and that it was a supreme achievement to discover the power and release it.

Jesus tried so hard to make this point clear to those who followed him. Again and again he claimed that he was not a miracle worker, but that they themselves were the miracle. Their faith was the hidden power waiting to be released. He urged persons not to exaggerate the effects, but rather to discover the cause. Nevertheless, unimaginative people missed the point that Jesus made. It happened then, and it happens today. So it is that the process of prayer, so evident in the life of Jesus, is largely an undiscovered resource of mankind. Modern man still clamors for miracles, unaware of the fact that the miracle is within him. Man alone can discover these resources and set them free to bring to reality his inner kingdom of power, love, and light, that more abundant life of which Jesus spoke.

10. PRAYER AND GROWTH

WE have expressed the viewpoint that prayer is an experience of growth. These who observe the growth process note an element of mystery everywhere evident in nature. Geological studies reveal the slow growth of the earth, the raising up and wearing down of mountains, the building up of alluvial plains and river deltas, even the slow growth of crystal structures. The astronomer gives his account of the growth of the stellar galaxies. The botanist tells the story of the slow growth of the giant sequoias and of the morning glory with its short-lived beauty. The biologist describes the morphology and function of living creatures ranging from the one-celled amoeba to the mammal with its billions of specialized cells. Beyond all such descriptive accounts is the mystery of causation, only a small portion of which can be comprehended.

One look at a newborn baby reminds us again of the infinite potential bound up in a few pounds of living, wriggling matter. Not the least of the wonders is the pituitary gland, which stimulates physical growth toward its fulfilled pattern, and then wisely knows when to call a halt before the creature becomes a giant.

Much of our culture is geared to mental growth. Formal education is structured to transmit to each generation the working knowledge of prior generations. We are told that a youth at sixteen has as much basic mentality as he will ever have, but the processes of education work to awaken his mental potential to the point of realization. Intelligence is measured as the ability to accomplish useful ends. So education not only provides knowledge but provides skills whereby knowledge can be put to use. Beyond this, education allows a place for personal achievement, for it is the integrating power of the individual that transcends knowledge with wisdom. Wisdom is certainly one goal of education, but it is discovered rather than taught.

The elements of wisdom come from within the being of the person. They are always more than can be learned from books or laboratories. The wisdom we speak of is a depth perception into life that organizes facts and experience into a creative whole.

This creative wholeness cannot be achieved without spiritual growth. Spiritual growth calls for concentration, developed sensitivity, and a belief in the self that makes it possible to use the resources of self for the highest form of personal achievement. Physical growth depends on the glands and proper nutrition. Mental growth comes through education and experience. Spiritual growth, however, is a personal responsibility and a personal achievement.

It is distressing to see a mentally and physically well-developed person whose spiritual growth is stunted. Yet, without the discipline of a prayerful approach to life many persons exist at a level hardly beyond that of highly endowed animals. Spiritual growth, while not a lost art, has been sadly neglected in our culture.

Spiritual growth starts with desire. More often than not the desire is arrived at negatively. Persons back into spiritual interests because they have found their lives meaningless, a desert place devoid of beauty and purpose. Often the incentive for spiritual growth awakens during the period Carl Jung speaks of as "second adolescence." At age thirty-five the course of one's life is set. A man has then tasted the fruits of his efforts, and experienced the deadening effect of occupational routine. How can he escape the smothering effect of life's monotony? Some relief seems possible if he can rediscover the self that is in captivity. Some men will seek in adolescent fashion to rediscover those ideals and goals that point in the direction of spiritual fulfillment. Increasingly, persons nearing retirement age are filled with a desire to reactivate the mothball self that has been isolated and ignored through the so-called productive years.

Desire leads to concentration, the intensification of thought on the sole object of study, the spiritual being that would be stimulated into growth. The discipline of concentration can be mastered by anyone of serious intent. At first it may be disconcerting to realize how restive our minds tend to be. All too frequently they are like Mexican jumping beans, popping from one thought to another without internal control. Simple devices can be employed in exercises to strengthen the power of concentration. One might for instance pick up a pencil from the table and focus thought upon it intensively. No rival thought is to be entertained. Intruding thoughts are immediately dismissed from the mind. Early efforts may succeed for but a few seconds. But with resolve and practice the time span will lengthen to the point where the mind will respond in obedience to our will and command. The pencil may open up a whole world of related interests like manufacture, materials, and uses. Thus, through so simple a device we can learn how the mind can function when it is activated by willful control.

Prayerful concentration does for the self what the focused thought does to bring the pencil into more interesting and valued existence. The focus of attention upon a problem brings illumination and understanding of the problem not previously experienced. For example, a person may have difficulty with a business associate. It may be a general irritation rather than something specific. If allowed to develop it might cause a serious breach in human relations. Considered prayerfully, the problem would be examined to see why irritation is felt, what the roots of it are, and how they might be wisely managed. This leads not only to self-understanding but also to an understanding of the other person, and the behavior options that could be employed to improve the relationship. It might be discovered that, unconsciously, traits of a former relationship have been transferred, or that the praying individual has projected his dislikes of things within himself upon another who reflects the same undesired traits. Prayer, then, brings to the foreground and illuminates the relationship so that it can be modified.

This kind of cultivated understanding produces increased

sensitivity. When a person has probed deeply into his motives, he is on guard against being led astray again. He has acquired a higher level of personal maturity. Spiritual growth has taken place. One of the benefits of prayer as a stimulator of spiritual development is that the understanding of other persons tends to make it easier to get along with them, to accept them as they are with an appreciation of what makes them speak and act as they do. It is difficult to become threatened by a person who has been carefully held up to the insights of prayer.

When we have achieved skills in concentration and sensitivity in our relationships with others, it is interesting to see how our own lives are modified. We feel more confident in ourselves, and walk among others with more concern for their real selves and less apprehension about our own. We show the marks of spiritual growth when we are willing to accept ourselves with good will. Often we are our own harshest critics and most demanding taskmasters. Without realizing it we often punish ourselves for the very things we would willingly accept in others. Prayer helps us to believe in ourselves as persons of value. The reciprocal benefits of this are quickly observed, for as we grow in understanding of others we more easily accept ourselves. Conversely, as we are more comfortable with ourselves we become more comfortable with others.

Prayer then becomes the growing edge of the spirit, the point at which we use concentration, sensitivity, and self-understanding to grow beyond our prejudices, fears, and immature emotional traits. Time reserved for this venture of spiritual growth is well invested. It stimulates further growth toward the goals of maturity that are essential for the achievement of true selfhood. This, too, then is a part of the process of prayer.

11. PRAYER AND THE GREAT AMPHIBIAN

❧❧

THE process of evolution teaches us some important lessons. The long slow process of developing lungs marked the great step upward in evolution. The achievement of the first amphibians was to be able to live both in water and on land. The ability to take oxygen from the air instead of the water marked the advance in mobility that made it possible for creatures to possess the land.

The limitation of growth in the insect kingdom was due to the fact that the skeletal structure was on the outside, and the internal development was limited by it. The emergence of creatures with skeletons on the inside made it possible for growth to reach new levels of size and variety.

Eilhard von Domarus, the psychiatrist-anthropologist, made a study of the tree and land apes and found that the ability to develop versatility was important to those modifications of the anthropoid that led to the development of the characteristics we associate with higher forms of life, the antecedents of man.

Sir Joseph Needham, the British biologist, in his book *The Great Amphibian*, makes it clear that the rapid development of man was made possible by his ability to live in both a material and a spiritual climate.

The great breakthroughs in the evolutionary process have come when a creature was able to move beyond the environment that had limited his growth, and step with confidence into a new environment that encouraged further mutation.

Man with his spiritual endowments has the capacity to develop resources for understanding cause-and-effect relationships. This capacity rescues man from bondage to materialism. But as with the history of evolution, man's progress has been marked by costly experimentation, trial and error, failure and success. Timid creatures have retreated from the prospect of such a breakthrough. The risk of frontiersmanship calls forth the fears of added responsibility. Conservative and radical tendencies appear in the evolutionary process as well as in the lives of individuals.

Pitirim Sorokin in his study of genius has pointed out that the traits of the genius are mental endowments that have strong psychic resources. The genius knows by some kind of instant insight what others have to work hard to develop. He feels that telepathic sensitivity cannot be ruled out as one of these resources of the genius. When we face these unusual powers we often try to interpret them in terms of usual mental endowments. It is difficult to explain the higher by the lower. A child prodigy, for instance, exhibits mental powers that are not easily explained. The capacity strikes like lightning and cannot be predicted. Nevertheless, when it strikes it cannot be denied. We have been so conditioned to the importance of laboratory science, where results can be predicted and controlled, that we feel uneasy in the presence of unpredictable deviations. Yet, to deny their existence is just as unscientific. On occasion, we may deny the results of our generally reliable instruments. The story is told of a man in Easthampton who opened the box containing his newly ordered barometer on a September morning in 1938. When he saw it pointing to an unbelievable low of 27 inches he assumed the mechanism was faulty, reboxed it, and took it back to the post office. Two hours later the most destructive hurricane in years hit eastern Long Island. The barometer was accurate; the incredulous man erred in his judgment. The inclination to doubt the spiritual sensitivities of the great amphibian, man, persists.

The point at which man seeks to rise above his material nature and fulfill the possibilities of his spiritual endowment may prove to be the next great evolutionary breakthrough. Instead of denying his spiritual consciousness as a hazard, man might use it as a corridor to lead him to new frontiers. The creative identity of man with his cosmic counterpart through prayer becomes the integrating process whereby his higher nature is acknowledged, exercised, and developed to the place where it is the dependable foundation for being and action.

Man's knowledge may produce fragmentation. As he increases his knowledge of minutiae, he limits his capacity to see the overview, or communicate effectively about it. Three Ph.D.'s who were preeminent in their respective fields of industrial chemistry, analytical economics, and micro-organisms were thrown together at a social gathering. After unsuccessful efforts to find points of common interest in their fields of specialization they gave up and spent their time in small talk. Their special knowledge had insulated and isolated them. Even their specialized language became a barrier to communication. The research scientist grows increasingly lonely as he finds fewer and fewer people able to share with him his special interest. In our world of specialization this development is not only discomforting, but threatening. If no point remains where people can share the qualities of their humanity, social disintegration may be so complete that destructive forces may gain control due to the default of man. In fact, man's highly specialized but fragmentary knowledge may disorganize the spiritual unity so essential to a healthy communal life.

Never before in history has the hazard of disintegrated knowledge been so acute. Never before have men been faced with the possibility that their achievements might so disorganize their lives that there would be a breakdown. No one can have a comprehensive enough grasp of human achievement at the intellectual level to make it possible to organize creatively the fruits of knowledge for man's common good.

It is more important than ever before that some sound basis be established for restoring man to his proper role. It is here that the developed spiritual consciousness may provide man with salvation. Salvation is the point at which man is saved from nihilism. If man can be saved from the disintegrating force of his knowledge by the integrative power of his quest for meaning and purpose, he will be able to rise above the threat of destructive knowledge to the use of creative understanding.

Jan Christian Smuts, in his advocacy of a philosophy of Holism, points the way toward a way of life that finds a focal point above conflicts of interests where cooperative efforts can be realized. Professor Kropotkin, in his study of the mutual-aid factor in evolution, traces a tendency as marked as the competitive struggle which makes it possible for conflicts to be resolved at a higher level. If the philosophy of Holism can fulfill the possibilities of the tendency toward mutual aid in the evolutionary process, there is new hope for mankind.

It is our belief that prayer as the instrument of insight and understanding, as well as the process by which personal and social integration can take place, affords man the most effective means for moving beyond the stalemate of this stage of evolution. The mind enamored of its materialistic achievements needs the discipline of a force that gives meaning to collective effort as well as individual enterprise. Only when the disciplined mind finds social and cosmic purpose sufficient to sustain its efforts, can those efforts guarantee healthful and creative action.

The great amphibian takes full advantage of its creatureliness. At the same time, he reaches toward the Creator searching for clues to the meaning and purpose of life. Finally, the ultimate worth of any effort will be preconditioned by men of integrity and high purpose.

12. PRAYER: MAN'S SUPREME COMMUNICATION

OUT of the varied elements of prayer that we have examined there emerges a process which engages man's total being. It is a relationship of active encounter, a spiritual dialogue through which questing man seeks out every possible meaning for his existence.

This dialogue with cosmic proportions is more than an exercise in language, for language is but a symbol to serve in the communicating of ideas. Language is useful at the beginning for prayer to assist the beginner in developing communicative resources of spiritual quality. In learning any language the first stage is facilitated by translating the unknown into symbols with commonly accepted meaning. In the first steps of prayer our mother tongue, our known language, may serve as a starter crutch, a point of departure. We soon discover, as we advance in the prayer process, dimensions or modes of communication that exceed the narrow confines imposed by words.

It is important for us to realize how much communication moves beyond words. A facial expression, a gesture, one's attitude, the pose, a sense of awe and wonder—all function without dependence upon words. The highest moods of man resist captivity by the best manipulators of language. The preparation for this act of supreme communication which invites the reorganization of thought calls for an inner calm, an uncluttered presence which is as ready and willing to listen quietly as to speak.

How seldom do we take time to relax completely. Our tensions constrict the muscles of the body. Emotional unrest affects the body chemistry and promotes the symptoms of illness. Turmoil of mind frustrates every effort at clear thinking and self-improvement. The preparation for this supreme communication requires relaxation at the deepest levels, not merely the deliberate untensing of the muscles, but also just as careful an attention to the freeing of the mind and emotions from conditions that restrain them from responding to the higher sensitivity that is the goal of this communication. There is a deliberate effort to bring serenity into the core of being, so that calmness, peace, and quietness exist. This is not escapism. Rather, it is face-to-face encounter with an ever greater reality that usually escapes us.

Sometimes the preparation for this supreme communication calls for an emptying of one's self of bitterness, anger, and hostility. There is no safer place to do this than in prayer. The Biblical admonition to "Curse God and die" was born of deep insight. Often the anguished, fevered spirit is so torn within that it cannot find any true point of communication until it vents its anger, pours out its troubled feelings, and purges its system. The cry, "My God, Why?" has been the prelude to much true prayer. When deep feelings break loose and there is no human whose love is great enough to bear the burden of unfettered abuse, the love of God may be most evident. The nature of God's love is that it continues to care even when we do not. The outpouring of a healing despair is often the prerequisite for restored faith. It is important to note that the Twenty-second Psalm, a psalm of great anguish of spirit, was the prelude to that sublime utterance of faith, the Twenty-third Psalm. There is therapeutic value in making prayer so basically real that no portion of the being is concealed. Calmness and peace within come to those who pierce the wound of the festering spirit.

The therapeutic values of prayer come as the vision clears, reason is restored, and right feelings begin to take the place of despair and anguish. It is important for us to have a safe place individually and collectively where we can examine the worst freely so that we can see the best adequately. The mood of prayer is one of open and complete honesty where the blunt and painful truth is faced squarely with the knowledge that only the truth can set one free.

We seldom take time to look squarely at our self-admonitions. We abuse, condemn, belittle, and ridicule ourselves in a manner that would grossly offend others. In the process of prayer we can look candidly at our failures and shortcomings with the knowledge that this is not the end but the beginning of something better. This prayer is not further self-abuse, but is rather the honesty that is the prelude to self-acceptance. In the depths of prayer the important thing is not what we say to ourselves, but rather what we are ready and willing to let God say to us.

At this point, prayer becomes the instrument of our whole being in finding its wholeness. This is the way we lift life-experience to a higher level of contemplation so that it is integrated about the claims of the spirit rather than about the foibles of the flesh.

Jesus illustrated the significance of this supreme communication in the Garden of Gethsemane. He was engaged in no mere verbal exercise, and his disciples claimed that he sweat blood. He brought the claims of his physical existence to the place where they were measured by the highest will he knew, and there he found the verification for the spiritual meaning both in life and in death.

This prayer of supreme communication is quite obviously not so much something you do, which implies a partial engagement of being, but is rather something that you are, which calls for the investment of the total being. It involves a special type of thinking, where the mind is made the agent of the being in a quest for meaning that is often beyond the merely rational. It is the point at which the claims of the spiritual nature place their demands upon the totality of life. Then no part has the right to intrude its claims upon the whole, but the totally integrated being marshals the resources of body, mind, and spirit to fulfill its highest, God-revealed purposes.

This type of prayer practices the discipline that keeps opening the way for more and more spiritual insight and spiritual experience. It is not a matter of time and place, form or ritual, but is rather the achievement of relationship between creature and Creator that opens the floodgates of full spiritual consciousness. It can make the creature responsive to the world about him with feelings of awe, wonder, unity, peace, goodwill, and inspiration. It can lead him to stand equally in awe and wonder of that inner kingdom whose deep recesses are exposed and illuminated by the processes of prayer.

Unfortunately, many persons live and die without being aware of the fact that they have the capacity for spiritual communication. Like those whose eyes are blinded or kept shut, the illumination of the spirit is not a part of their experience. Organized religion is frequently at fault for allowing people to think that they have found the meaning of prayer in the formal liturgical acts of public worship. However, the individual must feel the importance of his own priesthood as he is aware of his own nature crying out for its life. Even the mood of our scientific era makes possible the acceptance of a deeper mysticism that finds in the wonder of creation a counterpart of the wonder of being.

This supreme communication is the achievement of a relationship of oneness of being between creature and Creator, so that the possibilities of the spiritual nature are fulfilled in the actualities of the spiritual life. Here in this ultimate integration of being, social purposes, scientific knowledge, and personal needs can find their fulfillment through the realization of ultimate meaning.

PART THREE

The Discipline of Prayer

❦

13. RELAXATION

❧ ჰᎮ ❧

WE have stated repeatedly that prayer calls for self-discipline. Anything as important as prayer places significant demands upon life. An athlete trains until his muscles work at maximum capacity to respond to his will in the game. The musician trains to achieve a coordination of mind, muscle, and mood in the perfection of his art. The physician practices his profession that his skills may be in top condition to meet the needs of his patients. The person who would achieve mastery of the significant form of human endeavor we call prayer shares the need for study, practice, and disciplined effort.

The prayer that helps man draw closer to his divinely endowed nature is made possible by a deliberate and sustained effort to produce the mood that is conducive to it. The creation of the proper moods for spiritual growth requires discipline. One of the prerequisites is relaxation.

Freedom from the variety of tensions that plague modern man sets the right mood for responsiveness to the prayer act. You may object to this in view of those times of emergencies when you have felt the need for prayer, but found relaxation to be impossible. This is undoubtedly true, but the effectiveness of prayer in an emergency is an indication of the skills that have been developed in times relatively free of tension and crises.

The word relaxation is misunderstood by many people. One commonly gets the word picture of a free-and-easy state where cares are brushed aside and tensions flow out of our bodies.

Our use of the word is quite different. Relaxation as a prelude to prayerful thinking is not inert. It is the essential power of repose. Great creative efforts are the product of a repose of spirit that lays the basis for action. We can see this energy-in-waiting principle in the steam locomotive puffing gently as it awaits the signal to pull out of the station. Here is power in repose. Or, observe the jetliner at the end of the runway with its motors idling, awaiting clearance for takeoff. Here is tremendous thrust power awaiting its release. An athlete who has learned the power of relaxation is able to use his energy and skills more effectively when they are needed.

For many persons effective prayer is always out of reach. These are the people so engrossed in themselves, their inner conflicts, and states of tension, that they cannot rise above them. Their lack of purpose and self-discipline multiplies the trouble spots almost to the point of hopelessness.

The disciplined use of creative thought processes needs the strength that comes from repose. I remember hearing a relative of Sergei Rachmaninoff tell of his preparation for periods of musical composition. I had thought that he would sit down before the piano and experimentally try notes, chords, and melodic lines until he had found what he wanted. However, quite the opposite was true. He took his score sheets and went into the forest where in solitude and isolation from routine activity he could be receptive to the music that was stirring deep within his mind and spirit. Then with a rush of inspiration he would record the notes upon bits of paper, and hurry home to play the score and test its quality against the quiet inspiration that gave it birth.

Relaxation is the creation of the condition where the self can be brought together with quiet but undivided purpose. How do we create that state?

First, how do we relax our bodies? The mind has control of the nerves that direct the muscles. These muscles are the focal point of tension. We sometimes stop suddenly to take stock of our muscular state and find that we are rigid and taut. The mind can quickly remedy this by speaking to the muscles in order, telling them to relax. Starting with fingers and toes one can work up through his muscular system until he has changed the muscle tone of his whole body. It is important to remember the two sets of muscle that account for a disproportionate share of our tensions. These are the muscles of the lower jaw and diaphragm. With the deliberate freeing of our muscular system from its rigidity it is interesting to note how a feeling of quiet well-being pervades the rest of our being. This makes it easier to bring repose to mind and spirit.

It is erroneous to assume that the most uncomfortable physical postures are essential to prayer. In liturgical worship kneeling or standing for prayer may be prescribed. In private prayer, however, the position least likely to produce distracting physical stress or discomfort is that of sitting upright with both feet flat on the floor and both hands resting on the thighs. One can sit in this position for long periods of time without distraction or fatigue. The tensed body expends energy needlessly, the relaxed body conserves energy for creative use.

How do we relax our minds? The mind with its unique ability to focus on one thought at a time is a wonderful instrument. It can serve you well if you are its master, and can cause misfortune if it gets out of control. Fortunately our minds are so designed that we are free to choose the focus of thought. Here the learned arts of concentration are useful, and they can be developed so that the mind is freed from anxiety-creating and worry-producing thoughts. Doubtless you have known persons with minds preoccupied with morbid and calamitous thoughts. How different life could be for them if they had conditioned their minds to serve as a storehouse of the good and the beautiful. Devotional reading of the great spiritual classics, quiet contemplation of beauty, truth, and goodness can relieve the mind of tension and let it focus on the material that is conducive to spiritual sensitivity.

How do we relax our spirits? Our spirits are the core of our being. If they fester with poisonous feelings and attitudes, the rest of life soon becomes contaminated. In quiet understanding we can disassemble our anger, bitterness, resentment, and self-pity, and we can reconstruct in their place the wise and healthy emotions of love, patience, self-acceptance, and goodwill. We usually experience trouble with our spiritual natures when we seek to dethrone God and manage the universe on our own. The inescapable consequence is that we become judgmental and critical of others. If we can bypass such anarchy and accept the fact that we are members of a large organization, we can withdraw in composure from many of our falsely assumed responsibilities. We will find that both we ourselves and the universe are much better off for this recognition of divine sovereignty. Only when we stop playing God can we find God.

A British publisher brought out a book for business executives which was to help cure what he called "Americanitis," or a frenzied rushing through the day. He recommended an hour a day in quiet and uninterrupted meditation. Time so invested, he claimed, would make all of the rest of the day more productive. It would be reorienting time, to find out what was going on deep inside. It is not only a good antidote for "Americanitis," but it is also a clear hint as to the value of a relaxed, reposed approach to life.

Relaxation then is a first step toward the mood that can make prayer a fruitful, disciplined procedure. It is preparation time, growth time, and reorganization time. This approach to prayer does not merely use time to do something, but more important, it opens the way to become somebody or, more significantly, some mind or some soul.

14. RELEASE

A concomitant of relaxation is release.

Perhaps you have had the experience of starting off in your car with the emergency brake engaged. The car did not seem to have its usual power and lugged along. The odor of hot asbestos provided the clue as to why the car came to a bumpy standstill. All of the energy of the car was blocked by the tenacious insistence of the brake system. The power was there, but unfortunately the driver had acted at cross purposes. He had neglected to release the brake.

We understand mechanics better than living. All too often we try to advance through life with our brakes engaged. The end result is that we are thwarted, blocked, and often come to a standstill. All too quickly, limitations are accepted uncritically, suffering is responded to stoically, and failure is believed to be one's inevitable fate.

Certain releases must take place before we can share the benefits of forward motion in living. The ancient prophets prophesied the coming of one who would bring release to Israel. Jesus spoke of his ministry as one that would bring release to the captives. But the captive ones are not necessarily those in corrective institutions. The reference includes those who have built for themselves dungeons of doubt, and fortresses of fear. We need not only to be released from imprisoning ideas within ourselves but also the ensnaring ideas around us. Release can have a positive aspect as well. We can be released to something better, for something more worthy of our natures.

How do we find release from imprisoning ideas through the discipline of prayer? We already know that the negative emotions are the great taskmasters. They handcuff life and put the ball and chain about the ankles of their victims. These negative emotions are fear, doubt, suspicion, self-pity, guilt, hatred, and despair. When they lay hold of life they lay waste to it. Bitterness, resentment, and ill-will poison the wellsprings of existence, and often produce serious forms of mental and physical illness. A physician called me saying, "I am sending a patient over to talk something out with you. He complains of a gnawing stomach pain. I find no physical cause for it but I know he cheated his sister out of her part of an inheritance about six months ago. I think he is suffering from a guilty conscience." The man arrived and we talked the problem through. He admitted his guilt and made the proper restitution. Then and only then did the gnawing pain disappear. The pain was real, the guilt was real, and the restitution was essential to right the wrong that had been done. His very system cried out against the negative emotion he harbored.

When these damaging emotions in giant proportions take hold of life they imprison the minds and spirits of their victims, and only sufficient corrective action can set the captive free. Prayer may well be the instrument of insight into what is enslaving the self, and by following the insight that comes through a prayerful examination of one's action and attitudes the door may be opened to corrective action. Jesus pointed out that the process of worship has prerequisites. He said, "First be reconciled to thy brother, and then go and offer thy gift upon the altar." The gift without the spiritual commitment of the giver is a poor substitute for the self-giving that releases the person from his damaging emotions.

But not all of the imprisoning forces are exerted from within. We are all subject to subtle social forces that breed prejudice, critical judgment of others, and false standards of success. False ideas of what it means to be good may be a brake upon life. With self-pride a person may list the things he does not do as if this is a tribute to his virtue.

Jesus had hard words for people who tithed their salt and pepper but refused to face the weightier responsibilities of spiritual concern. Often persons are so blinded by prejudice that they fail to see the spiritual endowment God has invested in other human beings. In their efforts to justify their inadequate judgments they distort scriptural truth and violate the very basic conditions for right relations with others.

Persons also need release from wisdom that is not wise. False standards of what is true can become a hazard to discerning action. The uncritical acceptance of political platforms or organizational programs may distort the larger responsibility of the person who would see life clearly and see it whole.

There is the clear-cut need to be released from false ideas concerning health. Sometimes we accept physical conditions as unalterable when by the use of our directed spiritual energy they could be changed. By an overemphasis on physical symptoms rather than upon the reservoir of health, life can be gotten out of focus.

Sometimes we need to be released from false ideas of patriotism, for it is too easy to overlook the claims of conscience when the flag waves and the bands play. Ultimate spiritual values are seldom lifted up in the market place or in the houses of parliament. The individual who values conscience and spiritual responsibility finds them more adequately in the quiet of his place of prayer.

Even false ideas of what it means to be a Christian can so enslave persons that the basic teaching of Jesus may be unacceptable to them. Those who feel their faith is verified by believing absurdities merely remove themselves from the larger truth that could be theirs.

At many points in our society we need to be released from false ways of thinking so that we may be free to find the truth.

But release is not merely to escape from what binds life to personal inadequacy or cultural lag. Release may move toward positive goals. A balloon cannot ascend until its sandbags are unhooked. But when it is set free from the restraining weight it has something within itself that wants to take off into the upper atmosphere. Prayer can set men free to find that quality of being that is at home in the upper reaches of the spirit.

Prayer can point the way toward release through the grace and forgiveness that comes with God's renewal of time and opportunity. Release can come to the cramped and imprisoned life through a new awareness of the meaning and purpose of existence. Release can come through the feeling of unity with the Divine Nature.

The point at which prayer becomes the channel for this release from the negative emotions of life and freed to respond to the positive feelings comes in the quiet perception when man measures himself by that which is more than himself. The social insight comes when he measures the claims of society by the higher sensitivity of spirit that judges society as an extension of the self, and thus not free from the obligations a person would place upon himself. The point of release is found when the mind of man is measured by the divine wisdom that is revealed to him in quiet contemplation.

The famous mystics of the past have held up the ideal of complete self-denial. This should not be interpreted as self-abnegation which downgrades the value of the individual, but rather as the ability to detach one's self from the negative emotions that easily possess and enslave life so that the attachment to God and his will, as reflected through the positive emotions, can be achieved.

15. RELATIONSHIP

IN the discipline of prayer, relaxation and release serve their main purpose when they lead to a spiritually sustaining relationship. The whole purpose of prayer is to stimulate and bring to fullest reality in the mind and spirit of the one who prays the creature-Creator communication. This relationship is surrounded by the mystery that is implicit in so many of the meaningful bonds of life. No one can penetrate the mystery by which light rays through an electrochemical process are turned into sight. But seeing is an essential relationship of the being with what surrounds him. No one can explain the mystery by which sound waves in air are transmitted through a liquid by three tiny bones to a solid without loss and become comprehensible. A multitude of sounds surround us and add meaning to life. We live continually with life-sustaining mystery through the relationships that connect the inner man with the outer world. The mystery of relationship through prayer may be different in kind but it is not different in quality from the incomprehensible forces that add meaning to life.

Different persons achieve their response to the relationship of prayer in different ways. Saint Augustine found resonance of being. Saint Thomas Aquinas found support from a complicated logical system. Saint Francis responded to a rich source of meaning he found through feeling. John Wesley found his response through the relationships that were experienced. As with any relationship, the significance is determined by what is related by the attitude of prayer.

In the relationship of prayer, man, the creature, deliberately and with assurance accepts his creaturehood, the full wonder and mystery of it, as the first requisite step toward a fulfillment that lies both in and beyond that creatureliness. Many persons never take the first step toward prayer because they never accept the full measure of their creaturehood. They deny it directly and indirectly. They want to be somebody else. They want to be somewhere else. They want to have something else. This denial of the reality of themselves and their world leads them on a false and elusive quest. The essential of self-acceptance is to start with yourself where you are. One cannot enter into the relationship of prayer by proxy.

The quality of self-acceptance determines the nature of the creature-Creator relationship. Whether it will be friend to friend, slave to master, or spirit to spirit depends on where the relationship starts in the mind and emotion of the praying individual.

Often persons sing lustily, "What a friend we have in Jesus" and then unthinkingly add a most unfriendly quality to the relationship by singing the next line, "All our sins and griefs to bear." What kind of a friendship is it that avoids responsibility by putting it on another, no matter how willing? Friendship is at best an achievement of mutuality, not an escape from responsibility.

In Christian tradition there has been a tendency to accept a master-slave relationship, with self-abnegation on the part of man and glorification of the nature of God. This is another easy escape from responsibility which has no warrant in the attitude or teaching of Jesus. He wanted men to rise to their full spiritual stature and achieve the possibilities of divine sonship.

The relationship of prayer seeks to find the highest possible basis for friendship in the spirit-spirit communication. This calls for mutual acceptance, a recognition of a partnership in the management of life. It assumes that God is a spiritual power and man a spiritual employer of power.

The relationship based on the spirit-spirit encounter does not deny responsibility and does claim a mutuality. An heir is one who has a valid claim to the inheritance even though he usually comes a generation later in time. Man's achievement of spiritual sensitivity may have come later in time but it is of a quality that makes the relationship show the marks of equality. This is not a form of blasphemy but rather an effort to accept the challenge of the New Testament.

When Jesus spoke of the relationship that existed between himself and God he said, "I and the Father am one." We immediately note that he used a compound or plural subject but a singular verb and a singular predicate adjective. Here the meaning seems quite clear, for the creature and Creator are one in quality though separate in identity. The discipline of prayer is the effort to bring the separate entities into a relationship made possible by the common spirituality. Man does not become God nor God become man by the exercise of the relationship, but the capacity for God-consciousness in man, and man-consciousness in God becomes actualized in spiritual communion. It makes possible a relationship in nature without loss of identity.

When this relationship is achieved it makes possible the clear focus on the creative self. This makes available the power for self-integration, for the multiplicity of selves accept the sovereignty of the spiritual self. Right relationship with God through spiritual communion brings right relationship within the self for the anarchy of selves is resolved.

This relationship for man involves an act of will, an act of intellect, a use of the power of choice, and the investment of the total being. Saint Paul spoke of achieving the "mind of Christ," and this represents the act of the intellect, as the divine impulse supports the act of will. Both are expressions of a life-sustaining, creative faith that underlies the relationship.

Perhaps we could best think of the relationship of prayer as a subject-object bridge. A bridge is a very special kind of architecture. It is built in special places for special purposes. It is designed to relate things that otherwise would be separated. Nothing seems more purposeless than a half-demolished bridge that goes nowhere and connects nothing. Bridges bring together functionally what is separated naturally. So prayer bridges the gap between creature and Creator by bringing together functionally what otherwise would be separated by the qualities of materiality.

Prayer as a specialized state of consciousness moves the being beyond the usual considerations of real or unreal, conscious or unconscious, organic or inorganic, subjective or objective, to the place where he is dealing with the totality of being at one and the same time in a way that produces sensitivity to the whole. As George Russell put it simply, "Human evolution is the eternal revealing of the Self to the selves." The relationship marshals the resources of the selves and directs them toward that point of revelation where the Self is made known.

In the processes and disciplines of prayer a bridge between the selves is built upon which the Self may stand and looking both ways may better bring about the unity of the diverse and separate. For it is always the function of the bridge to unite those entities that desire to be together and which find their finest meaning only when they are together.

The subject-object relationship is achieved then not only in kind as spirit speaks unto spirit, but also in quality as the best in the being responds to that in the cosmic order that sustains it and gives it meaning.

So prayer may well be called the highest function of the self that is seeking in its unity to find the fulfillment of the selves. In this unity the body may find its health, the mind its meaning, and the spirit its peace.

16. RECOGNITION

AT the common everyday level of experience we know what recognition means. We may unexpectedly see a familiar face in a crowd and instantly we are flooded with recognition. Not only does the eye see but the feelings respond and action ensues. If it is a friendly face we may be filled with pleasure and call out to attract attention. If it is an unfriendly face we may be overcome with unpleasant feelings and quietly try to get by unobserved. The recognition that is part of the discipline of prayer is something like this common human experience raised to its highest degree.

Recognition is a contribution of the praying individual, which he initiates. It is seldom an act devoid of preparation. The familiar face is recognized because in prior experience many events and feelings have been related to it. The spiritual recognition that comes with prayer may be a rush of insight, but it is usually built upon the acts and attitudes that make it possible. The exception would be when we recognize what others have described so effectively that there is no doubt in our minds as to what it is. If you have never seen Niagara Falls, you may approach the falls with the desire to see their grandeur. Your ears may pick up the thunder of the cascading water before your eyes see the river, but when the falls come into view there is no mistaking them. The recognition is the product of preparation without direct experience. So it is that there are times when our achievements in prayer are built on our anticipation which has grown from the study of the experience of others. But even here the praying individual is the initiator, for directly or indirectly he has prepared the way for the moment of illumination.

The disciples of Jesus shared such an experience on the Mount of Transfiguration. It was the moment at which the large truth was grasped instead of a number of smaller, more easily grasped facts. The disciples had become familiar with Jesus and his ministry. They knew about the events of his baptism, temptation, preaching, and healing. They had seen him influence the lives of persons so powerfully that they were changed in attitude and action. But they had also seen something else taking place. They had been aware of a growing opposition, a more vociferous dissent from official quarters, and a marked thinning out of the crowds that came to hear his preaching. The throngs dwindled from thousands to hundreds, and even the disciples had misgivings about the apparent failure of the ministry of this man to whom they had so willingly attached their hopes.

Jesus knew what was seething in the minds of his disciples. He also knew it would be difficult by any ordinary device to explain to them the meaning of the course of events. He needed their understanding, but if his ministry was to be carried on they would need to understand the meaning of events. He announced to them that his ministry was soon to end because he would be put to death by enemies of his cause. Having made this disclosure to his disciples, he selected the ones that he thought were most mature spiritually and took them up to a mountain spot. There he quietly disclosed to them the meanings of life and death. He showed how Moses and Elijah had achieved great power through the way they died. He explained his mission, his love of life, his desire to live on, but his responsiveness to God's will as the first claim upon him. After he had interpreted history and events in his own ministry a great wave of recognition swept over them. The scriptures tell us that Jesus was transfigured before their eyes, and his physical presence took on a spiritual aura. It seemed that even the clouds of heaven worked to verify this spiritual insight that came with their recognition of a truth that was more significant than a series of facts or events. They shared a moment of great knowing which was to change the course of their lives.

Jesus knew and the disciples soon proved that this moment of recognition would have to be supported by disciplined effort. While they could not live as if this moment of transfiguration had not happened, neither were they completely removed from their human weaknesses and inadequacies. When they returned to the valley persons called on them for healing and they failed because, as Jesus reminded them, their faith was small-sized. But this period of illumination, brief as it was, as tenuous as was their grip upon it, became a source of reassurance for them when they had to carry on the ministry of Jesus alone in an unfriendly world. The recognition with its illuminating quality touched more than their minds, and their deeper nature was never to be the same again.

The act of spiritual illumination is not commonplace. It does not come on schedule or upon order. But those who make careful and patient preparation may have that moment come to them when with a burst of insight their deep capacity for God-consciousness may be fulfilled. Some theologians claim that man has an instinct for God, and that his spirit is restless until it finds itself in relation to God. We can observe how powerful an instinct can be when we watch ants and bees at work. We can see instinct at work in the skill of the oriole building its swinging nest. Here is a power beyond reason that is verifiable by observation. The untouched powers of man's spirit when brought to a moment of recognition may so empower life that it is transformed.

There is a small bird that summers in the Aleutian Islands and migrates in winter to Hawaii. According to scientists there is no known way by which the tiny muscles of the bird can store enough energy to keep its wings in motion for the long overwater flights, but the birds go on doing it with sure confidence that there are sources of power available to them that are beyond understanding. According to accepted theories of aerodynamics the bumblebee is too large and heavy to be sustained in flight by the wings he has been provided by nature. But the bumblebee does not know that and so he goes serenely about the business of flying, using resources that are beyond explanation. But the power is always the product of a relationship fulfilled.

Within the spiritual nature of man there are resources of power that can be let loose to flood life with insight and understanding. Some persons might deny that such powers can exist, but the person who has experienced the flooding of life by them is as unconvinced by the doubts of others as the bumblebee or the migrating bird. For what we are dealing with is not so much a matter of verification as of experience.

At the core of all creation there is a divine purpose at work. In a moment of divine recognition where the depths of our being are revealed to us we gain understanding that moves us beyond the common distinctions of freedom and determinism, animate and inanimate, subject and object. We become filled with the recognition that beyond the conveniences of the devices of thought there is an integrating meaning that is known, felt, and experienced.

Sometimes the moment of recognition comes as a religious experience. At other times it may creep up quietly and unexpectedly, to lift us up to a moment of cosmic consciousness where our feeble human equipment is supplemented by a comprehension we do not grasp or easily interpret.

For many, to look into the face of Jesus and grasp the fullness of the meaning of God's power in human form is the ultimate of recognition. As with the disciples on the Mount of Transfiguration, order grows out of the confusion, faith emerges from the doubts, power is made available to the weak, and there is hope for the despairing. But the spirit must live with expectancy if it is to find the moment of recognition with its fullness of meaning.

17. REASON

OFTEN there is a question as to how reason fits into the disciplined life of prayer. We use reason as the abstract term designating the product of reasonableness. The reasonable is hospitable to reason and makes a proper place for it in the total life of the individual. Prayer should not deny or violate reason, though it may transcend it.

Prayer as an instrument in finding ultimate truth should aid the seeker in finding it. Pilate represented the legal mind when he asked Jesus, "What is truth?" George Fox represented the religious mind when he led the Society of Friends in their search for spiritual truth. Both must have been aware of the fact that truth is never fully found through reason, though it is equally true that it is not found by ignoring reason.

Reason is compounded of at least three elements, diligent self-examination, ceaseless critical inquiry, and docility before facts.

It is the nature of the reasonable person to keep continually in focus the aspects of his nature that might inhibit reason. Sometimes strong emotions intrude upon the life of a person so vigorously that they overwhelm reasoning powers. It is difficult for a parent to be completely reasonable with his own child for his emotional involvement is so great. It is difficult for the intensely religious person to be completely reasonable about the institution to which he has given his loyalty. The reasonable person takes these matters into account and makes doubly certain that proper allowance has been made for these strong feelings.

The reasonable person also has the searching mind that is engaged in ceaseless critical inquiry. In a Midwestern community there are persons who make it one of the major tenets of their religion that adherents believe that the earth is flat, no matter what explorers and scientists have to say about it. One of the leaders of the cult made a world cruise to prove that it was flat. Upon his return, he reported that no matter where he went it looked flat to him. Such persons could not be thought of as given to ceaseless critical inquiry. The fact that they take a religious document that reflects an outmoded view of the universe and impose it on the present without regard to discoveries of the past few hundred years places their attitudes in an irrational pattern. One does not have to go that far to find evidences of lack of critical judgment. To judge a whole group of persons by the characteristics of the few is equally irrational. The person who values reason makes a strenuous effort to examine facts and adjust his attitudes to them.

The reasonable person also accepts an attitude of humility before the facts. To deny the validity of the structure of reality in the smaller expressions of it usually indicates that a person will be poorly equipped to deal with the larger dimensions of reality.

When reasonable attitudes are abandoned in either direction trouble is certain to result. If persons too quickly deny reason because of their prejudices or ungrounded emotions they produce fanaticism and delusion. Those persons who periodically sell their homes and possessions and gather to await the end of the world as predicted by signs and prophecies create a fanatical faith and then abject disillusionment. But to make such a fetish of reason that there is no other dimension for life may be equally disappointing as a person becomes unimaginative and intellectually muscle-bound.

The resolution of the problem comes at the point where reason serves man's spiritual nature through the discipline of prayer. Reason brings together two kinds of truth, the truth of the senses and the truth of revelation. The truth of the senses is explored by the organized knowledge we call science, which works within its own limited and limiting method. The truth of revelation uses the total being as a channel and so cannot be bound by a limiting method.

It is important however to realize that some of the processes of revelation are at work to develop the skills of the senses. Seeing and hearing, for instance, are learned processes, and because of the revelation of experience each of us sees and hears differently. The skilled ear of the symphony orchestra conductor has developed a different range of hearing values from the person who has never developed a musical sense. The eye of the artist sees color values where the untrained eye looks in vain. So, even the equipment of the senses that we use to verify the truths of observation varies with the products of training and experience that have helped to form them.

The truth of revelation employs intuition and something more, for the whole being is employed in the response. It uses not only the senses, the emotions, the resources of intellect, but also the capacity for believing which is a measurable ingredient of the mind's life. Reason then becomes, as it were, a secure launching pad for the flights of spiritual sensitivity.

The discipline of prayer brings into a working synthesis the truths of the senses and the truth of revelation, and uses each to check and verify the other. Neither is completely adequate in and of itself. A scientist who is so enslaved to mere facts that he has atrophied his imagination will not go far in the rarefied atmosphere of modern scientific inquiry. Nor will the devotee of prayer, no matter how stimulated his imagination, produce much that is valid if he separates himself from the verification of reason and careful observation.

Reason aids us in seeking the relationships between cause and effect. It is concerned with answering the question, "How?" As we gain understanding of the cause-effect relationships of life we gain security in relation to things. The mind is geared to the security reason helps to furnish. So while reason is essential to the proper functioning of the mind, it is also the suitable antechamber for the flights of imagination which are produced by sensitivity of spirit.

It is important to remember that what is true for you can be modified by what you let happen to you. Your point of view determines perspective. The proper use of the mind and its endowment of reason can help to make secure the foundations for disciplined prayer. Prayer helps us bring together firm fact and dependable intuition.

In man's evolutionary development reason came late and followed after emotion, intuition, and instinct. The value of reason is that it brings to a higher point of refinement the more primitive endowments of man, and subjects them to a measurement and control that is important for their best function.

Reason is a tool. A tool is useful only as it is used for creative purposes. A hammer can be used to build or to destroy. Its value is subject not to its own inherent nature, but in the way it is employed. Reason can be a burden or a privilege. It can be used as a tool that blocks the higher aspirations of the imagination and spirit, or it can be used to direct and guide these subtler endowments toward their finest realization.

The disciplined mind is essential to effective prayer, because any resource as powerful as the spiritual endowment of man deserves the full benefits of careful direction and wise use. But as with any instrument, its value is determined not by its existence, but by its use. In the higher refinements of prayer, the powers of reason can always be used to serve the needs of the spirit.

18. REALIZATION

❦

REALIZATION designates the quality that can make things real for you. It points to the ability to make the abstract concrete, the imagined within reach, and the envisioned attainable. There is greater frustration than satisfaction in knowing that there is a spiritual kingdom prepared for you if you are unable to move forward to possess it.

In the discipline of prayer the final testing comes at the point of total commitment, complete willingness to act on the faith factor. It comes to us where we are offered the pearl of great price and then cry out in consternation, "I believe, help thou my unbelief."

The cynic claims that every man has his price, and that every man's integrity can be compromised if his price is met. We learn from shopping expeditions that money values predominate in the world of things. The shopper checks the price tag, and then decides for himself whether the price is right.

When we have learned as much as we can about prayer theoretically and abstractly, we come to our moment of truth. We decide whether the way of life available through the discipline of prayer will be worth the cost to us in changed patterns of thinking, feeling, and action. Prayer as we speak of it is not so much a spasmodic or occasional activity as it is a complete commitment to a demanding way of life. We are faced with the question, Will it be worth the cost? Am I willing to invest enough of myself to bring about the realization in my being?

What will it cost to make the realization of the life of prayer possible? It will cost all that you are and have. Unless all of life is made subject to the discipline of prayer, the benefits may easily escape us. Jesus explained the costs clearly to his followers. He pointed out the dangers of partial commitment that compounded the inner conflict and left the person worse off than when he began the pilgrimage. He showed that the distractions of life can easily obscure the ultimate commitment. Therefore, preoccupation with property, industrial equipment, and family must be avoided. He likened the great commitment to the merchant who specialized in fine pearls. One day this merchant saw the perfect gem, inquired as to the price, and found it so great that he would have to liquidate all his holdings in order to buy it. Since this was the dream of his lifetime, the end of his quest for beauty and perfection, he committed himself, sold all that he possessed, and bought the prized pearl. Jesus goes on to point out to his disciples that the choices concerning things are temporary, but the choice concerning one's soul is eternal. What benefit would accrue to a man who might accumulate enough of the world's goods to fill several warehouses if he should suddenly find that the gift of life entrusted to him was neglected so seriously that it was taken back by the giver of all life? That man's possessions would be of no value. Foolish indeed is the man who is so confused as to values that he devotes his time and energy to getting things which are damaged by moths, eaten away by rust, and stolen by thieves. He has created problems for which he has found no solutions. The wise man works to build a kingdom of inner values which is permanently safe from corrosion, contamination, and confusion.

The cost is great but how does one determine whether the benefits are worth the investment? Again Jesus pointed out that the value can be established only by acting upon faith great enough to make the commitment. The person of double vision is handicapped because he does not know which of the two objects he sees is real. He is confused, and stumbles through life in a worse state than the blind man. "But if your eye is single your whole being is flooded with light." Clear vision at the point of life's values brings everything into right relationship.

What does the life of prayer demand in personal commitment? It places the demand upon life that every act and attitude be lifted up for examination before the highest self, the spiritual being. It demands that life be kept sensitive to the revelations of God's will and guidance that can come through the cultivated awareness of prayer. It demands that the individual be ready and willing to accept the awesome burden and responsibility of spiritual power that may be let loose in him. It also means that he must be prepared to act as he prays. This can be a frightening responsibility unless one has made complete self-commitment. Imagine asking in prayer that your spirit be made pure and sensitive and then face the responsibility of acting as if God had done his part and was waiting for you to do yours. Over the door of an Eastern college library there are words, "He who reads and reads and never does is like the farmer who plows and plows and never sows." It is equally true that the life of prayer must eventuate in action or it reechoes the feeling that it is false and deceptive. As the life of prayer is a projection of faith in the spiritual nature of man, it is also a demand upon life that this faith be acted upon, for only as the prayer is sustained by a self-verifying act can the faith be justified.

There is always a hazard in trivial or superficial acceptance and partial commitment. It is the hazard of the person who stands at a point of decision and cannot decide which way to go, and so tries to go both ways at once. He is torn apart in the process. It is a disintegrating action and the whole being suffers the consequences.

The disciplined commitment of the life of prayer directs the energy of the whole being—body, mind, and spirit—toward the highest form of integration, the fulfillment of the quest of life for its meaning. Then the values that are really valuable, that have meaning beyond the measurements of space and time, become uppermost in life and the trivial price tags that are set on things stay where they belong, on things and not on people.

What is true for the individual in the discipline of prayer can also be true of the nation that seeks its destiny in spiritual leadership. It can put its trust in supersonic planes, in hydrogen bombs, and atomic-powered submarines, as the warriors of old put their trust in horses and chariots. But this basis for trust is deluding, for it creates the very fears and moods of conflict that it was intended to alleviate. Massive retaliation, overkill, and obliterating striking power are familiar terms in our day, but they say nothing to the spiritual aspirations of men. They deny not only the spiritual endowment of our so-called enemies but by a destruction of values so contaminate our own thinking that we are reduced to valueless creatures with the master planners of destruction calculating the casualties in the tens of millions. The placing of trust in things so destructive is the ultimate and final act of blasphemy for it would willingly destroy from the face of creation the only God-conscious creatures that ever lived in order to preserve things that ultimately cannot be preserved by material power but only by spiritual power.

The matter of complete commitment at the personal level produces social and national obligations that we cannot escape. The disciplined life of prayer permits no place for man's destructive attitudes toward man, nor can it give status to the outworn prejudices that would measure man's value by the standards men set rather than the endowment God gives.

The recognition of the price the way of prayer demands of life is a prerequisite to the commitment, for it is a far-reaching act of self-giving. But the act of faith involved produces also the ultimate of self-finding.

19. REJOICING

WE too easily adapt ourselves to the idea that the dedicated life is a diminished life. We accept the principle that to deny one's self is to punish the being in order to gain questionable advantages. We confuse pleasure with joy because we have all known brief and pleasurable sensations, and are not likely to have had the experience of true joy.

Prayer as we approach it is the ultimate in personal fulfillment. It brings to life the quality of self-realization that is the source of true joy. The endless quest for pleasure misdirects the energy of life by aiming the search toward satisfactions that may be good in themselves but not good enough to reveal the ultimate meaning of existence.

A young woman richly endowed with physical beauty came to the end of her days by a suicidal act, leaving the message, "I have tried everything and find that life is not worth living." Physical satisfactions alone have a point of diminishing return and do not lead a person to that point "where true joy is to be found."

A wealthy, highly respected man, when being congratulated on his eightieth birthday, said, "Many persons think I have had a good life. I have done some good things and I have accumulated lots of money. But I know I won't live much longer. I have invested my life energies in the things I must leave behind. In all honesty I must admit my life is a failure. When I was young I wanted to be a missionary, but I lacked courage. Nothing else has ever satisfied me." When one denies the major commitment of life, no substitute is ever quite good enough. Some deep inner standard keeps passing its self-judgment, and no one can ever get away from himself. True joy is to be found only when the best self finds its way to fulfillment. Nothing less is able to satisfy the depths of being.

Perhaps in human experience the sensations of love at the physical level are meaningfully contrasted with the realization of love at the spiritual level. A pleasurable feeling comes when an appetite is satisfied, but this is far from the sacrificing, demanding, often painful responsibility that is assumed with an all-consuming love. Theodor Reik in his study of love and lust says:

L'amour in French comedies is obviously not the same as "love" in Holy Scripture. . . . Did not psychoanalysis deal fully and penetratingly with love? It did not. It dealt with sex, but that is something quite different. . . . It is not restricted to expressing an emotion between the sexes, but also expresses the emotion between members of a family. It signifies the feeling for your neighbor, for your friend, and even for your foe, for the whole of mankind, for the home, social or racial group, nation, for all that is beautiful and good, and for God himself.[1]

Satisfaction of the appetite for sex can lead to satiation and frustration. The demands of love may lead to suffering and failure, but the depths of being are so released by the process that even the suffering may become joy-filled. This is not as contradictory as it may seem, for it is only when all there is of a person is committed to the highest goals to which he aspires that he knows the fullness of being. Only when this fullness of being is realized can a person become aware of the meaning of true joy.

Our age with its increase of leisure time has given itself increasingly to a quest for pleasure. Artificial risks are incurred in gambling, hunting, and racing. Artificial stimulation of the human body is produced by the use of stimulants and drugs. Vicarious entering into the experiences of others through reading of novels, dramatic presentations, cinema, and television make it possible to become aware of experiences without actual participation. All of this means that the ability to enter into life for one's self, to gain from it the deepest meaning, is forfeited by an endless quest for synthetic or substitute experience. No wonder there is an increasing sense of frustration, when days and years are dissipated in artificial living rather than in direct participation in the realization of being. True joy can never be found in the artifacts of life but only in the achievement of fullness of being. This is possible only when the commitment is properly directed. Fullness is never achieved by way of escape, substitution, or the use of vicarious experience. Fullness results from our finding the true self, and exer-

[1] *Of Love and Lust* (New York: Grove Press, 1959), pp. 9–10.

cising the full potential of this true self by making real the encounter of the fully actualized self with the full possibility of existence.

It is at this point that the discipline of prayer keeps turning persons away from the substitute toward the actual, from the escape to the encounter, from the artifact to the real.

The joy of self-discovery brings together all of the elements of the process of prayer plus the disciplines of prayer. It becomes a growth that knows no limits, for the more that is discovered, the more there remains to be discovered. The growing edge of self-awareness activates capacities and sensitivities that were dormant or unknown. Just as the student of nature finds more and more of wonder, the deeper he explores and the more he knows, so the person who plumbs the depths of his spiritual nature finds wonders within his being that are stimuli to the further exploration of the inner kingdom.

The rapidly expanding insights of the psychologists provide challenges to those who would find the fullest meaning of their own selfhood. Capacities of mind and emotion recently explored verify the wonders of the inner kingdom that is waiting to be discovered and developed. To limit life to the physical and intellectual denies to life the higher integrating experiences that can be known only when spiritual fullness is realized.

A cosmology that has long since been outgrown is an inadequate basis for a theology or a psychology that illuminates the spiritual self and the praying self. No longer can men turn with satisfaction to a God "up there" or "out there." The inner kingdom as the dwelling place of the divine nature was made explicit in the New Testament, but has remained unrealized as long as men keep seeking it where it did not exist. But the discoveries of the psychologists fortify the will to discover the full dimensions of the spiritual kingdom that has long been ignored, the kingdom of God within.

Part of the discipline of prayer essential to self-realization comes with the courage to look beyond the outworn cosmologies and theologies to the realm of exploration and discovery that lies within the capacities of consciousness. The mood and attitude that is willing to seek where the seeking can be fruitful, to discipline where the effort can be productive, is the basis for growth in the understanding of prayer as a way of life and an expansion of the very consciousness that is the special endowment of man. To do less may provide pleasures, but it can never open the doors to the expanded consciousness that is the realm of true joy.

Because the ecstatic state is rare we have been inclined to think that there is something abnormal about it. But the true ecstasy that comes when the potentialities of spiritual awareness becomes fulfilled in the actualities of spiritual responsiveness is the highest experience the human can know. This disciplined quest for the finest meaning for life, demanding and sometimes painful as it may be, brings to man the nobility bound up with his highest nature. Then he no longer lives merely to satisfy the appetites that are an aspect of his physical nature, or to realize the truth that is essential to the stability of his mental life, but building on both he moves on to possess the promised land of spiritual fulfillment which brings his capacity for consciousness to the place where it transforms life, and sets firm the foundation for the experience of rejoicing when deep speaks to deep and is answered.

PART FOUR

Prayer and the Dimensions of Selfhood

❧⊱⊰❧

20. PRAYER BEGINS WITH GOD

❦

THE dimensions of selfhood are bounded by the degree of cosmic meaning attached to life. The greater our understanding of the nature of God, the greater our capacity for giving significance to the part of creation we are. Prayer is the language that acknowledges a beneficent power in the cosmos with which a personal relationship can be established. It is evidence of spiritual expectation. It grows deep within the self and moves beyond the self. It fulfills deep emotional needs and realizes high spiritual possibilities. In fact, it is the very ground of our being.

Small gods produce small ideas of prayer. Remote gods make the struggle for relationship strenuous. Gods related to currently untenable cosmologies place a strain on credulity that makes these gods remote or ridiculous. The gods above or beyond are geared to an age past, and have no more possibility of personal meaning than the idea of the sky as an overturned bowl upon a flat earth. The nature of God that challenges the best mental and spiritual ventures of modern man is the God of the New Testament. This God can be found within the being, can become the very basis for being, and can provide the capacity for consciousness and the justification for our existence as spiritually responsive creatures. Such a great and challenging approach to God opens the way for great and productive prayer.

Man's idea of God has developed through the centuries from that of a capricious dispenser of favors to a creative law-making and law-abiding power. Our idea of prayer then must progress along similar lines and change from that of the beggar's outreached hand to the search for and fulfillment of the deepest demands of being. This prayer then makes firm the grounds of being, both personal and cosmic.

How is prayer affected by our subjective ideas of God?

Ten persons will look at a picture and have ten different reactions. The objective reality of the picture remains the same, but the subjective response differs according to what each one brings to the picture.

Ten persons will think of God in ten different ways depending upon their backgrounds, training, and experience. The objective reality remains the same but the subjective response differs.

Obviously the subjective concept may be inadequate and distorted. What we are and what has happened to us may cripple our thoughts. A youth about to be sent overseas on a military mission went to his chaplain to discuss his uneasiness about his unbelief in God. He said, "I would like to believe in God. I would feel better about going across if I did, but the idea of God as Father goes against me."

The chaplain learned that the serviceman's father was cruel and vicious. Every time this youth heard the word "God" he had a feeling of revulsion. The coupling of the words "father" and "God" made God unacceptable to him. By way of contrast, there are many other youths for whom the word "father" means a loving, kind, just, and wise individual. For them, the use of the word brings a rich meaning to their idea of God. The meaning we impute to an abstraction is a projection of our own personalities. The meaning of God for us is never separated from what we are and what we have experienced.

The effort to develop an adequate concept of God is probably the greatest venture of mankind. It has challenged the most perceptive and tenacious of minds. As with children disillusioned after being told that Santa Claus is a myth, so also is the disillusionment of the adult whose concepts of God remain at childhood levels. Maturity in the God concept comes through a long and strenuous growth process from which evolves a belief so grand in scope that it brings maximum meaning to life. The process itself infuses the seeker with a capacity for relationship that must be fulfilled. Such persons can affirm with Saint Augustine, "Our heart is restless until it repose in Thee."

The Christian conviction about the nature of God is not an accidental by-product of life or something automatically bestowed upon us. It is an achievement of a disciplined mind and spirit through which we seek to invest life with the highest possible meaning and purpose. The search engages the total personality. There is tragedy in any life that fails to grow to normal size, but there is nothing more distressing than those spiritual "Tom Thumbs" whose religious development is retarded and stagnated at the childhood level.

The Christian idea of God has been clearly defined in the teaching and attitude of Jesus but this idea was not born full-grown. A brief survey of the Biblical accounts will indicate the changing trends. The writer of Genesis pictured God as a wizard who could call a planet into being. In Exodus he was delineated as a meddler in the affairs of men. Throughout the history of Israel he was seen as a taskmaster, a tactical warrior, a vengeful overseer. The prophets saw God as a judge meting out punishment. Amos pictured him as a loving being—but with mortal qualities. And Jesus? He demonstrated to us that God is the creative spirit of good—a God of love and a God of law who functions through man for the ultimate good of all creation. He also taught that the universal spirit can be individualized in the life of man. "I am in the Father, and ye in me and I in you."

The mature believer knows several things about God. First

of all, God is dependable. This is basic to his ethical nature. God is revealed to man through law and order, the inviolable relation of cause and effect. The structure of the universe as we observe it is undergirded by this dependability. The tragic results of broken laws cause us distress, but they tend only to accent and verify man's assurance about the orderly nature of the cosmos.

Men respond to this world of dependable law in many ways. The astronomer is filled with wonder at the precision of movement of the heavenly bodies. The physicist regards with awe the intricate structure of the atom. The musician is challenged by the laws of harmony and their endless variety of expression. The master of the graphic arts is inspired by the law of perspective, composition, and color. The saint's devotion, the sage's justice are bound up with an ability to respond to a higher order within the cosmos. They are built upon a belief in the dependability of God.

We also identify God with creative good. The evidence is abundant. Man is born with an innate urge to improve himself and his world. Consider the healing properties in the human body—pulling us always toward the "norm" of perfection. Healing properties in the earth move it also toward restoration after the holocausts of war, earthquake, fire, and flood. Recall the implacable force of life which causes a small seed to expand with the strength that can split a rock. Surely also it is significant that man achieves his greatest satisfaction in creativity, whether it be planting a garden, cleaning a floor, or composing a symphony. Another evidence of God's goodness is the delicate balance with which nature maintains life when even a few degrees of deviation in the earth's axis would mean annihilation of man either from burning or freezing. Probably the best evidence of God's nature and intent are the words of Jesus, "Be ye perfect as your Father in heaven is perfect."

This is the great tribute to the ideal of perfection in the inner kingdom where God dwells and we find the ultimate ground of being.

The Christian concept of God cannot be separated from love. Love is man's highest form of response and man cannot impute to God less than his own highest capacity. Love operates over and beyond reason. Love forgives seventy times seven when reason might allow less. Love produces a concern for, a responsiveness to others. It is positive interrelationship among humans. It has the same possibility in the Creator-creature relationship. Belief in a God of love answers man's deepest emotional need for it recognizes a cosmic concern at the center of reality. As the latest studies of human personality verify life's need for sustaining love, so it is revealed to the sensitive spirit that love is central to the idea of God.

The Christian knows that his relationship with God will lead him to ultimate truth—not as a distinction between fact and fallacy but as a vast revelation of the core of reality. In some mysterious way guidance and wisdom flow into us through prayer until we are able to convert absolute truth into concrete truths which invest our daily lives with integrity and moral purpose.

Man lives in a material world structured with hours and days, yesterdays and tomorrows. His civilization has progressed in proportion to his ability to make consciousness work for the convenience of our nature. But God is not so bound. The eternal is beyond measurement or the need of it. The eternal does not violate the laws of measurement—it is simply beyond our capacity to measure. We use words to point a direction beyond our capacity to measure and in that beyond is the nature of God. We may approach understanding but we can never arrive as long as we remain in our finite framework.

Because of our love and faith, our prayer life conveys us

into the unbound realms of the spirit and there finds the "fatherness" which is its source. Reaching God with acceptance and affirmation is the supreme act of man's spiritual nature.

When we regard God in this way, then the burden of answered prayer falls upon us. God wants a perfect person and a perfect world through us. But he has given us the freedom to choose or not to choose perfection, and the freedom to learn or not to learn how to attain it.

Now let us look closely at the self which knows so well how to ask—but so poorly how to receive.

21. PRAYER USES THE SELF

WE have looked at prayer as the God-given capacity of the soul for spiritual communion, innate and beyond measure by the yardsticks of science. When the Psalmist cried out, "My soul is athirst for God," he was expressing the mood of the mystics, and attitude of saints, and the universal feeling of the God-conscious soul.

Let us turn to the roles we play as praying creatures. One of the important problems of modern thought is the nature of the self. For centuries man felt he knew who he was and what he was. Now he is not so sure. Statistical studies reveal one image of man and explorations of the unconscious show quite another. The stresses of history cause one type of behavior while man's response to religion causes another. Anthropological studies of ancient man reveal likenesses to and differences from modern man. Though there is a unity running through all of the explorations into the nature of man and his selfhood, there is no simple or conclusive answer that explains his behavior and aspirations. A number of recent books have dealt with the problem of selfhood from differing and partial approaches. Yet no partial answer suffices, for even the proponents of limiting theories about the nature of man feel within themselves that man is always something more than the sum of his parts.

What is this something more about man that cannot be isolated or defined? Some secular spokesmen say, "It is nothing. It is an illusion. It is false." But a series of negations do not satisfy the affirmative feelings that are a part of experience. The religious answer claims for man a spiritual essence that is the core of life's meaning. The soul, the vital principle, the transcendent meaning, according to the religious mind, is the true man. Here the capacity for self-consciousness exerts its influence on experience to produce something more than the total of experience. Here the nature of man builds on the capacity for rational thought a structure of meanings that raise life to its nth degree.

In the Christian tradition the self is an entity of special sensitivity that is able to respond to its spiritual counterpart. "You are the sons of God." "You are fellow workers with God." This special entity of the self is realized through seeking God's will and living in accordance with it. Therefore it cannot so easily be a mass action as an individual action. When life is motivated by this quest for its spiritual meaning, all of life is affected. John Wesley, after years of tortuous seeking, had an experience of self-realization that changed the course of his life, gave it direction and power as well as meaning. This experience of self-realization may be the best evidence in human affairs that God works through man.

This self-realization is not primarily an achievement. It is a fulfillment of innate capacity for spiritual sensitivity. As a bird does not need to be convinced that it can fly, so the human responds to a quality of being that is an endowment.

Yet what is innate is not inevitable. The potential self is seldom the actual self. An adequate self is the first essential of an adequate prayer life. The struggle for adequacy within the self is probably best indicated by the failures to achieve that quality of selfhood in modern life.

Though there is no such thing as a clear picture of modern man, there are clues to his nature. The essentially materialistic, mechanistic, and secular emphasis to so much of life shows how man regards his spiritual nature. The frustrated, thwarted, and confused life that many people live testifies to an orientation well below the spiritual potential.

If, as the Scriptures indicate, "our bodies are the temples of God," we have desecrated the temple. If our minds are instruments for insight into things of the spirit, we have made them feeble instruments. If, as units of energy, we are to respond to God and his will, we have misdirected this energy. If, as souls athirst for God, we seek to satisfy them with materialistic substitutes, frustration is the inevitable reward. Thus we picture modern man, confused, diverted, misdirected, preoccupied, and, worst of all, denying his own nature.

But that is not all of modern man. There is a reaction to the restlessness. There is a desire for direction as well as diversion. There is response as well as escape. New and serious efforts are being made to understand the soul and the praying self. A finer sensitivity to things of the spirit is observed even amid the plethora of things and material values.

The soul as a praying instrument is bound by its self-imposed limitations. This is no new insight. Jesus called it to the attention of the well-to-do young man who questioned him about spiritual values. The advice he received was that he should give up the self-imposed limitations that he had placed upon his spirit so that it might begin to function as it was intended to do. So, the all but lost art of prayer is bound up with the self that may have allowed its spiritual sense to become atrophied.

But man's finiteness does not prevent his awareness of the infinite. His relation to the material does not preclude the spiritual. There is a way of releasing the responsive self that becomes the instrument of creative spiritual relationship.

Yet this totality of awareness may be transformed from its potential to its actuality by a learning process. Prayer is a learned capacity. The disciples on the Mount of Transfiguration caught the vision of a potential power and felt a new level of self-realization. But they had to learn to relate that power and that insight to the realities of the valley. Prayer is learned by doing. Even though we may accept the validity of prayer intellectually, we do not begin to pray until we have organized our living so that we pray as we believe and believe as we pray.

This learned capacity is the culmination of a demanding discipline. It is not a take-it-or-leave-it proposition. Rather, it is an achievement born of great mental and spiritual effort. It is the pearl of great price for which we willingly make a sacrifice. The reward is the abundant meaning revealed through the achievement of such spiritual unity and direction.

One does not need to be an expert to begin the process of self-discipline. It is sufficient to have a starting point and a mood of quest. The effort to use the self as an instrument in God's hands to do his will may move hesitantly and without certainty at first. But, taken a day at a time, the search grows in confidence. New awareness is born. The responding self begins to see, to hear, to feel, and to know new meanings. A peace and inner calm quiets the restless seeking and frees the mind to know and grow. The experience of the abundance of God's orderliness, his beauty, and his goodness begins to dominate life.

Wonder pours in upon life as it yields itself to the higher levels of living. Old things take on new meanings. New feelings are released that purge and elevate life. The self is being used for new levels of experience, and its response is a fulfillment. Formerly routine and ordinary activities of life are now transformed. Tedium becomes triumph.

Such an awakening of the spiritual nature is not solely that of ease and enjoyment. Strenuous reorienting in living is often required. One's old patterns of behavior, modes of thought, and feelings become strangely ill at ease in the presence of life's new meaning. But the self now at work in this creative experience of prayer is a higher self, and it must create the growth atmosphere most consistent with its new nature. Not infrequently the old habits and attitudes of the past must go.

Prayer uses the self, but only the self that is willing to be used. Prayer does not demand; it invites. Prayer does not compel; it proposes. Prayer does not overpower; it makes an overture.

Prayer may use you. It may add a new dimension to your life. This may be the day when you begin to experience the spiritual growth that comes when you begin to use your praying nature seriously. But the soul grows slowly. It responds to persistence and patience. And few there are who ever use their full potential as spiritual beings, made in the image of God.

22. PRAYER FULFILLS THE SELF

❧⟨§⟩☙

THE self is dynamic. It is alive. Experience is never just a matter of enduring. Something is continually happening to the self through its experiences. The self changes the environment of thought and feeling. But the self is continually involved in change by the quality of its own thoughts.

The self is no mere simple-as-ABC structure. It is a nature with levels of response, some superficial, some deep, and others midrange. What is done at one level affects the self at other levels of its being. What helps the self to fulfill the undeveloped portions of its nature at one level also penetrates other levels of being, and life can be profoundly changed through this process.

Prayer may not consciously recognize the interrelatedness of these levels of being, but such recognition is not essential to effect those changes whereby the being finds fulfillment at new levels of feeling and spiritual response.

In everyday thought and speech we encounter the reflected views of self-evaluation. When we hear the comment, "I don't feel quite like myself today," we recognize the evaluating self that passes a judgment upon the evaluated self. The admission, "I was nearly beside myself," indicates that there is a stable and an unstable element within our being. The confession, "I get angry with myself," reveals a self that feels and a self that reasons about the feeling. To say, "I am ashamed of myself," is to admit the quality of self that not only feels but also thinks about the feeling. In the response, "I forgot myself for a moment," we are recognizing that there is a self that controls and another self that is subject to the controls.

All of this means that whether we are consciously aware of multiple factors at work in our personalities or not, we unconsciously recognize their existence in our daily speech. Our task is to channel this recognition to the point of conscious thought. We shall then be able to sense the relationship that prayer can create among the selves.

At its least, the discipline of prayer brings to bear on life the power of the conscious, determining self to judge, to evaluate, to subject feelings to thought, and to measure all by an ideal of life set by an inner spiritual sensitivity.

One of the baffling problems concerning the self has been the source of this human capacity for the objectivity concerning the self. Without seeking to solve the problem, the act of prayer recognizes the possibility for this objectivity and uses it to modify life. Prayer is continually seeking to bring the lesser selves into line with the self that God intended to rule life. "Seek you first the Kingdom of God and its righteousness and all of these other things will be added unto you." It might not be amiss to say, "Seek you first the Kingdom of God in your self and fulfill its righteousness so that all of the other selves will be subject to it."

Recently a woman sorely troubled by a habit that was making a mockery of her life stood before a group of others who had been fighting the same problem of alcoholism and told how her lesser selves had been brought under the power of a self she hardly knew existed. Her way of life brought her to the mood of desperation. In that mood of utter hopelessness she knelt in prayer to ask for the inner resources needed to discipline and control her unruly self. At the very moment of her request she found the resources within her self to control and master the appetite for alcohol, and has been in mastery of that self from that day until this.

The quality of this kind of prayer is distinctively different from the vainly repetitious verbal exercise. It is a courageous discipline that isolates the false feelings. Real courage is called for when the light of intense honesty is focused upon the self. Yet, it is only by one's honest evaluation of the self, completely free of sham and partiality, that life can be integrated at its higher level. This becomes the act of fulfillment through prayer.

Jesus was uncompromisingly specific on this point. He fully understood the power of prayer and taught that prayer could change life. He knew the power of prayer to fulfill the best self. He knew that this power could be exerted in such a way that life would be modified at each level.

So it was that he urged men to pray for their enemies. Enmity is a dominance of the lesser selves at the level of human relations. This breakdown in human relations cannot be remedied by engagement at any of the lower levels. Increasing the enmity provides no cure. Self-justification offers no balm. And overt violence only accents its own futility.

What happens when these unruly emotions are brought under the control of a higher self, a self capable of praying for one's enemies? Enemies are considered as people. Their motives are understood. Suspicion and ill will are replaced by sympathy and concern. The incidents that have projected the enmity are seen in a new light. The motives are reexamined. Forgiveness becomes a possibility. Before long, it becomes a necessity. The enemy for whom one bows in earnest prayer ceases to be an enemy. The bases for friendship are created in the alchemy of spirit that can refine the dross to gold. It is not a form of magic. It is an employment of the higher laws of the mind that brings the lesser self under the subjection of the God-seeking self.

The same modifying influence can bring the fearful self under the influence of the faithful self. Fear with its disorganizing effect upon life can create a downward spiral of apprehension and suspicion of self and others. The fear-dominated life is filled with gruesome experience. The mood and attitude of faith can change the same external experience to an entirely different internal response. What has been feared can be accepted with confidence. The act of praying for sustaining faith can take the Gardens of Gethsemane and turn them into the triumphs of Easter.

The prayer that releases the faith-filled self is a life-saving influence because it restores to life the healthy perspective that fear has distorted. The faith-filled person keeps life in proper perspective. Trivia are accorded the small place they deserve. Important considerations get the priority; first things come first.

Thus we see that being fulfilled is being filled full of the best of life. This self-realization moves beyond the veneer of our lesser selves. Self-realization at the highest levels is intolerant of the iron curtains of deceit and falsehood that the unruly selves would use to thwart the spiritual self that awaits realization. But the prayer that brings a redeeming freedom to the spirit so that it may master life is not dependent upon piously worded formulas. Rather, it is an active struggle for values engaged in by the spirit that would know itself and be free. It takes no small discipline to free the finer self.

Something of the nature of this struggle for values is seen in the hidden story of Saint Paul. The conflicting selves within his being carried on a civil war that almost destroyed him. At first they led him to ruthless persecution of those whose ideas he could not accept. Then he succumbed to guilt feelings so great that he could not face himself and sought to escape into the wilderness. From the compulsive urge to destroy others, he turned toward self-destruction. After two secluded years in such self-immolation, a man named Barnabas came to him and helped him to talk through his conflict. It was then that he was able to reorganize the forces of his personality for constructive purposes. Thereafter, his life was freed of its false ideas and set on the road of great usefulness.

The power of a person like Barnabas lies in his ability to enable another person to see and understand the truth of the inner self. Such outside support of the better self helps it to come forth to realization. This imagination can be employed when a person prays with another or when he prays alone. When we pray with another, there is an identity that fortifies our best self. When we pray alone, we are truly not alone, for we are relating ourselves to a spiritual Other who is concerned with this spiritual realization and fulfillment. Whether another person is the instrument of fulfillment or whether our soul is released through a sense of identity with God matters little. What is important is that the inner conflicts and stresses of the person are released and the totality of life brought under its highest nature.

Paul knew the truth about Jesus but was unable to use it. A guilty self stood in the way and made his insight impotent. Then someone who believed in him more than he believed in himself changed the focus of his thinking and he was set free to use his energy and intellect creatively.

Wherever we look at the life and writings of Saint Paul we see the marks of his own experience. Until he could learn to control the direction of his own thinking; until he could, through a discipline of prayer, subject his feelings to a higher will, he was useless. But when his life was set free he talked of the peace of God that passeth understanding with all the confidence of a man who had a firsthand experience.

It is not difficult to think that Paul was talking about prayer when he urged his followers to "let your minds dwell on what is true, worthy, right, pure, amiable, kind and praiseworthy. . . . Then God who gives peace will be with you."

Just as Paul had been released from the troubled self, the limited self, the unfulfilled self, to find a new and valuable existence, so also can his spiritual descendants move beyond their impotent insight, their inner conflicts, and their fruitless struggle to personal fulfillment through prayer.

Perhaps we should examine the principle by which it works. The universe is ruled by laws. We do not break the laws with impunity. We can cooperate with them and find security. The laws of the mind and spirit are equally important for our welfare as are the laws of the natural order. We can develop the capacities of our minds and spirits to the place where they will respond fruitfully to the opportunities and privileges of our lives. We readily admit that "as a man thinketh, so he becomes," but we hesitate when we are asked to face the implications that are called forth in order to achieve personal and spiritual fulfillment.

Then the self that will be fulfilled through prayer will be a finer, a richer, and a more responsive life. It will be a self worthy of all the efforts that will produce it. We shall be those selves.

23. PRAYER TRANSCENDS THE SELF

WE come now to that more difficult aspect of prayer experience that we would call the transcendent response. It is beyond the range, domain, or grasp of human reason, yet it does not violate human reason. It is a surpassing experience that is not reducible to formulas or to scientific definition.

Just as life is dependent upon the proper functioning of the heart, but is not all heart, so the transcendent experience of the spirit utilizes reason but is not limited by it.

The transcendent experience is compounded of the needs and possibilities of the cultivated and responding spirit. It is not dependent upon understanding or definition, though that might be desirable. Just as we use electricity, though we have never been able to define it, so we respond to the transcendent experience of the spirit without requiring it to be defined. The experience is convincing enough, and description will usually suffice when inquiries are made.

Perhaps we can illustrate some of the formative elements of this transcendent experience. The great mystics have never been able to reduce to words their feelings of mystical response, but they have provided descriptive accounts that establish some general directions.

If we were to give an ordinary fuse plug to a bushman of Central Australia, we would get little meaningful response. He would lack the vocabulary needed to identify the object accurately. At best he might have some word that would imply a pretty stone or a shiny object. Nothing of the use, function, material, or purpose of the fuse plug would relate to his experience. Quite understandably, his reaction would be limited to his experience.

If that same fuse plug were given to a busy housewife, she would be able to respond immediately within her broader spectrum of experience and know-how made possible by identity and an understanding of purpose. In that respect her response would transcend that of the bushman.

If we were to give this same fuse plug to an electrical engineer responsible for research and development, we would get quite a different response. Immediately he would relate to it in terms of his understanding of its construction, its purpose, the problems of production, functional limitations, the nature of the fusing compound, and the many other factors that would be a part of cost, development, manufacture, and use. Because his experience had been so significantly related to the item at so many specialized points, his response would far transcend that of the housewife or the bushman.

So it is that the transcendent meaning reflects all that has been developed by the highest discipline to which the self has been subjected. But it does more, for it fulfills the latent endowment of the knowing person.

When the transcendent meaning is related to the sum-total response of a spiritually endowed and developed person, the possibilities of that response are the highest form of human experience.

Just as the bushman's idea of the fuse plug was limited, so also is the spiritual responsiveness of many persons. Having eyes to see, they see not, and ears to hear, they hear not. There was nothing wrong with either the bushman's sensory equipment or his natural endowment. It just happened that he had never been engaged in an activity that produced the type of knowing that could bring a fuse plug to the level of useful comprehension.

So it is that the person with a spiritual potential may remain a spiritual illiterate because he has never learned the language of communicating the feelings and needs of his spirit with the needs and feelings of his Creator. How seldom do we comprehend the reciprocal relationship that exists between man and God, and how little prayer means without it!

Even our creeds fail to illuminate this point. How much richer would be the sense of relationship if we would say, "I believe in God the Father and God the Father believes in me." "I believe in Jesus Christ, his Son, and Jesus Christ believes in me." There is little wonder that we are so ill-prepared for the experience of creative interrelation that is the basis for the transcendent.

Even those who are not religiously illiterate suffer a spiritual power loss when the mood of expectancy wanes. They know the power of God and the possibilities of prayer, but have not engaged both in an active partnership. Thus, what is intellectually possible may never come to experiential reality.

It is the saint who develops the capacity for relationship

to the place where it not only enriches his life but dominates it as well. It is the quality of the saint that he has practiced the personal experience of God and the response to God through creative communion so that he is able to experience the transcendent with confidence rather than fear. For him it is a "knowing even as also I am known." His epistemology then takes on a new dimension, for it is not alone what he can comprehend, but it is also how his spiritual potential can be used as a channel of that higher comprehension that becomes a revelation.

Then the life of the saint bears the marks of the achievement that starts with his inheritance, his endowment which is his instinct coupled with his culture; it adds to it his experience which is the dynamic response to the life he has lived; it relates it creatively to the given circumstance that is the act of experiencing in the present; and then it moves on from all three to achieve that which merges all in an unrestrained response to his own spirit as it is engaged in the active response to its ultimate. The saint can experience the transcendent meaning of prayer because he is so actively engaged in the expectation of it. He believes in it, he seeks it, and works to achieve it. When the experience comes he does not resist but yields to the full measure of self-realization that evolves through the experience of the transcendent.

When the human spirit stands before the transcendent experience of the soul of a God-conscious individual, it cannot deny the reality of the revelation that is produced. It may seek to avoid the implications or try to ignore the reality, but the experience of transcendence is as much a fact of life to the saintly as radioactive energy is to the atomic research scientist.

When the circumstances for this creative revelation are met and the creative interrelation of man and God is achieved, nothing that man can say or do can eliminate that stirring fact from human experience.

A group of learned ministers, physicians, and psychiatrists

has been meeting together for several years to try to understand and isolate those forces that they have observed at work in human experience. With the care of their respective disciplines they examine and eliminate all that will not fit the requirements of their minds. All are agreed that there are experiences that science can verify but cannot explain; experiences that challenge all present modes of thought about man and his nature. The power of prayer to heal and restore life, the power of the human spirit to have instantaneous knowledge and insight, the ability of the mind for communication across distances, and the ability to exert mental control over physical matter may be verified though not understood.

When this power is observed, it operates with such quietness and dignity that it seems more natural than unnatural. When called to the hospital to pray for a dying man who had been in a coma for two days, the pastor was accompanied by an interne and the family doctor. With one hand on the patient's forehead and the other clasping his hand, the pastor offered a brief prayer for the expiring patient's peace of soul. The pastor was as surprised as the physicians when the elderly gentleman instantly arose in bed and conversed freely and with complete lucidity for about an hour. Then with a smile he said, "I am tired and must go to sleep again." And he did— eternally. The physicians commented, "We couldn't have believed this if we had not seen it with our own eyes." But blessed are those who believe though they have not seen.

The demand for explanation often indicates that a person feels more secure standing in his own shadow than he would feel accepting the light of a higher insight. I do not need to know why I breathe before I take a breath. I do not need to know why I eat before I nourish my body. If we were always to wait upon explanations, we would die long before we had the answers. Nor is it necessary to know why I realize my soul's nature before I accept the privilege of prayer. The act is part of the answer, and the process is part of the goal. To wait for the goal to verify the process is illogical and destroys the very possibility of results before they can be experienced.

So this transcendent experience is not dependent upon logic though its very nature is supported by the logic of experience and personal fulfillment.

In approaching this endowment of spirit we may appropriate a method that has long been in practice though the words may seem quaint. Our spiritual ancestors spoke of standing under a conviction of sin as a prerequisite of the indwelling of the Holy Spirit which in turn produces the works of repentance.

The method is good in that it indicates a logical process, first, of getting rid of that which interferes with the operation of spiritual fulfillment; second, of getting something positive in its place; and third, of doing something constructive about the resulting experience. Too often we fail to experience the transcendent values of prayer because we become stranded at the lower levels of experience. To move quickly beyond that which restricts our spirits to the place where they are free to experience the communion for which they were made is essential.

But this does not call for repression or suppression. Rather it calls for expression. It engages the creative act of the responsive self.

Modern psychotherapy has tried to copy this ancient formula, but it has applied it in reverse. It encourages an expression of the worst so that the self may be purged with the assumption that it will then be free to realize its best. But the failure to make the best self realizable is due to the fact that the therapist usually operates with so limited a frame of reference that he cannot tell the difference between the sublime expression of a creative spirit and the diseased emotions upon which he so continually focuses his attention.

The quality of prayer of which we speak is not bound by the laws of psychotherapy. It is concerned with something more excellent than normalcy. It seeks to lay bare the transcendent reality of life so that the human spirit can stretch upward in ecstasy and delight toward the goals for which it was made. We are the sons of God and we were created in his image.

The self becomes more than the self when it is an instrument in God's hands. It then shares the transcendent experience of being.

24. PRAYER CHANGES THINGS

THE praying self that is fulfilled and becomes an active participant in an experience of transcendence cannot live in detachment from mundane affairs. His essential nature works its influence on everything he does. Thus, the praying self becomes an agent in transforming the lives of others that they may be drawn closer to the will of God.

In many homes of a generation or so ago there hung a motto, "Prayer Changes Things." The implication was clear: prayer was the key to power, self-improvement, and the better life. Then followed a period when persons felt that the phenomena of life had to be scientifically explained to be acceptable. The life of prayer no longer fit the patterns of easy explanation, and old mottoes had to go.

But, prayer is one aspect of experience, and all experience is a process of modifying life. To say that prayer can change things is no brash or mysterious boast. We know that thinking changes things. We readily admit the importance of careful planning. The imaginative thought of the scientist has captured the interest of most of us. The flights of fancy of a violin-playing mystic modified the life of our world even before those fancies could be verified. We quite readily accept the idea that thought changes things.

Meditation is a special type of contemplation where the focus is turned inward and upward. This prayerful type of thinking is not isolated from the rest of mental activity. It is a thinking process employed at a different level, and the modifications of life that it generates are likely to be revealed at a different level. So, logically, prayer changes things.

We have had demonstrated repeatedly how the power of an idea can change things that are essentially physical. Life may be made stable or unstable as an idea possesses it. Sometimes a brief conversation can exert such an influence upon a person's life that his moods and attitudes are changed.

Hypnosis has demonstrated that the power of an idea, once accepted, can change behavior. Carefully supervised experiments demonstrate how the physical strength of an individual can be markedly increased or decreased in actual performance, while the subject is under hypnosis. The temperature of the body actually can be changed through suggestion. Yet here we have no conscious effort, for the nature of the phenomenon is to have the ideas of one person speak directly to the preconscious mind of another in such a way that the desired response is brought to fulfillment.

If such a phenomenon is so easily demonstrable in hypnosis, is it not much more significant that the conscious mind is able to condition the content of its own subconscious levels of mental activity through carefully controlled thought?

Jesus seems to have had no hesitancy at this point. He said that whatever we asked in prayer, believing, would be accomplished. There were no ifs, ands, or buts. For him it seemed to be the enunciation of a principle of spiritual living. But he was not satisfied merely to state a principle. He demonstrated how it might be applied and then went on to say, "greater things than these shall ye do." The prayer that changes the subconscious ideas is the active agent in changing the things that are thereby modified.

It is strange that in our day the extravagant claims for the power of prayer come not from the clergy, who take a guarded attitude. The claims are presented by laymen of other scholarly disciplines whose thought-boundaries have been extended by an awareness of undeniable forces that laymen ascribe to the process of prayer.

A college professor of English literature, Glenn Clark, in writing about the botanist George Washington Carver, says, "Great as he is as a scientist, he is still greater as a man of prayer. Twice have I had the opportunity to pray with him in his laboratory, and I consider those opportunities greater than any opportunities I have ever had to hear him speak."

Dr. Howard Somervell, a fellow of the Royal College of Surgeons, but probably better known as the physician who accompanied the Mount Everest Expedition to its 28,000-foot level, writes concerning the treatment of a tubercular leg. "There was only one thing to do to save the patient's life and that was to amputate."[1] But the patient requested permission that he first go home and spend three weeks with his family. This was the result: "When he returned the leg was healed; he was able to walk on it and appeared almost well. A few months later he was completely recovered. The family and friends united in prayer seem to be the only reasonable explanation."[2]

[1] Leslie Weatherhead, *Psychology, Religion and Healing* (New York: Abingdon Press, 1951), p. 236.
[2] *Ibid.*, p. 240.

Dr. William McDougall, Professor of Logic at Oxford, in examining such phenomena writes, "Successful therapeutic suggestions and others that effect definite tissue changes from evidences above suspicion repeatedly warn us against setting up any arbitrary limit as to what may be effected in this way."[3]

Such modern men of the disciplined professions are simply restating in more modern words the thought patterns already expressed in the New Testament writings. We do ourselves a disfavor if we ignore their ideas and their spiritual implications. Our religious heritage has the potential power to transform our lives. To ignore the rich resources of that heritage is to impoverish life itself.

We hesitate to share with others our experiences of successful prayer because we consider such experiences to be far removed from normal life concerns. Yet people continually come to their spiritual advisers with evidence of the influence of prayer upon their own lives and the lives of others. The power of prayer is continually operative even though persons hesitate to bear their witness openly.

Sometimes the effects of prayer are so spectacular that they cannot easily be obscured. At other times they are revealed through a gradual modification of life that is barely perceptible. Sometimes they show up in the increase in understanding that gives more competence to living.

Probably most of the persons who came to Jesus would have been hard pressed to understand the rudiments of theology. But they received the essence of the faithful response, the expectancy that restored life. When we pray for the power that can change life, we must settle the question concerning the state of our expectancy. Then we shall hear, "Your faith has made you whole."

[3] Quoted in Weatherhead, *op. cit.*, p. 240.

Love, humility, expectancy—these three can work to bring about the changes in life. They are continually doing so.

In this two-way relationship that is involved in using the power God has given us we may be doing that which God can do in no other way. As Saint Augustine said long ago, "Without God we cannot. . . . Without us, God will not." Here is a working relationship wherein man's obligation to his Creator is completed in the act and the art of prayer. When the obligation is fulfilled, life is different and things are changed.

Yes, prayer can be an act of self-renewal. Prayer can be a form of action of mind and spirit that modifies life. Prayer can be a method by which the praying self relates itself to others so that their lives can be modified. The transcendent self, in God's hands, becomes a part of the active partnership wherein we are workers together with him. We can work with prayer or against it. The choice seems to be ours.

Whatever our choice, our lives will be affected by it in important ways. Denial precedes impoverishment. Fulfillment forecasts the experience of a changed life that can be instrumental in changing others. Truly, prayer changes things.

25. PRAYER CHANGES PEOPLE

❦

WE come now to the aspect of prayer that is most plausible and most practical, the power to change the lives of people. Often the course of life may be changed by a simple word, a

moment of illumination, or an experience of healing relationship. We seek to learn how this life-changing experience can
take place and what steps we can take to encourage and increase its influence upon the lives of others.

In our essentially materialistic culture with its secular emphases, our framework of accumulated experience is usually too
restricted to make room for spiritual considerations. The realm
of the spirit eludes the usual thought structures, so we are inclined to deny or ignore it. But the ferment of spiritual power
is too great a life force to be ignored or denied indefinitely.
We must come to terms with it.

Sometimes we can extend the boundaries of our experience
by a long, slow process of illumination. At other times, an un-
expected and perhaps dramatic experience of life bursts it wide
open with a surge of new insight. Whether our growth is slow
or rapid, it must enable us to rise to our full stature as spiritual
beings.

Sometimes even our ethical judgments seem to oppose or re-
tard our spiritual development. We hesitate to use our spiritual
powers when conflicting problems related to justice or judgment arise. Questions of conscience come to plague one. Why
pray for someone and neglect another equally needy person?
What should be the specific subject of one's prayer? To what
extent does our understanding of God's will control or limit
our prayers?

At this point we support the priority of the spiritual over the
ethical. The ethical structure is manmade, circumstantial, and
relative to tradition and culture. The spiritual nature is an endowment of God. Ethical frameworks can and do change. Spiritual realities are forces that work change. The moral values of
life represent man's effort to respond to God's plan for ethical
behavior. The spiritual response is the obedience of man to
the God-man relationship. If a priority must be established,
and often it is unnecessary and irrelevant, the endowment of

God should supersede one's human and natural desire to be wholly dedicated to ethical causes.

So, even those frames of reference that deservedly have gained religious sanction may on some occasions, and of necessity, have to adapt or even yield to the more direct revelation of spiritual reality.

How does prayer change people? Does it merely change the mode of their devotion and self-discipline? Or, does prayer condition the very core of their being so that others are convinced beyond doubt that a change has occurred?

In the prayer relationship deep speaks to deep. A conditioning process involving the mind and emotions is at work. The process is not identical for all who pray. Each personality projects its special qualities of being. But the conditioning process at work uses elements of the conscious to modify and recondition the lower levels of consciousness that are so significant for the shaping and determining of life.

The unreasonable and the disturbing elements in one's life are usually the invasive forces from lower levels of consciousness that erupt into patterns of emotional response and behavior. Saint Paul was concerned about the impulse to do what he did not want to do and to refrain from doing what he felt he should. His study of the life of Jesus led him to the place where he saw "All that he would but dare not be." As we pointed out earlier, it was the intervention of Barnabas, who acted as his psychotherapist, which released the unconscious restraints that guilt had fixed upon his life so that Paul was able to move ahead into his period of great usefulness.

The sciences of personality verify the importance of the reciprocal relationships that are at work in life. The moods of prayer that Jesus encouraged were actively engaged in fulfilling these reciprocal relationships that were in themselves life-changing. What a demand was placed upon life to "forgive as we are forgiven"! We are obliged to institute a reevaluation of our own attitude toward others before we can enjoy the fruits of the inner peace that comes with forgiveness. Each must answer for himself the question as to where the burden of responsibility lies for creating attitudes that cause human relations to become inflamed and festered. Peoples' lives have been markedly changed once they have learned how to forgive.

Perhaps all of this is predicated upon the ability to pray under the discipline of love, the mood of hope, and the undergirding of faith.

The New Testament equates God with love, not in any trivial emotional way, but in terms of his capacity for unlimited forgiveness, understanding, and good will. While prayer helps to create this mood as the premise upon which acceptance rests, it also is actively created by it as the discipline through which it is expressed.

The mood of hope is bound up with the expectancy of belief. The act of prayer is undermined whenever we approach its possibilities tentatively and with hesitation. If we truly believe, even in the smallest measure, the power of that belief projects itself into the realization of the result. The limits of our faith become the frame of reference within which our prayer is expressed. Small faith and small hope produce proportionate results. The daring spirit projects itself in great hope and great faith and reaps the reward in the spiritual powers thus released.

The mood of hope is made secure only when it is undergirded by a dauntless faith. This faith is not limited to selected beliefs, but is the response to God that loves with heart, and soul, and mind, and strength. The belief is faith at the intellectual level, the conviction is the faith at the level of emotional commitment, and the action that is the result of the conviction is faith operative at the muscular level. So faith works all through life as prayer must do also. For the prayer that does not eventuate in healthy action dries up the wells of inspiration, and the action that emanates from inadequate prayer is diffused in unworthy directions.

The power to believe and the will to fulfill, the ability to carry through in living the high expectations of prayer, unite to produce the greatest form of human discipline.

We cast our eyes back over what we have said, to recall that which can stimulate the active participation of each reader in the process and discipline of prayer which may produce changed lives.

The ability to live as a praying creature is an endowment, the gift of God. We have done nothing to earn it, but we have the obligation to use it.

The praying self as an instrument of response to God must work to fulfill certain conditions of preparation, concentration, and directed action. When that is done, the Beyond-Self unites with the endowment within the self to fulfill the spiritual possibilities of life. This fulfillment produces something that was not there before, and the creative act results in the transcendent quality of the responding human spirit.

The responding self cannot help but show the marks of the response in all that he is and does. So the world about him is changed as he changes. The power and direction of his thoughts show in the modifying of reactions and the stimulus to a new spiritual climate.

The praying church becomes a different church. The church that develops groups of persons dedicated to the discipline of prayer takes on a new vitality. The people in it see the marks of the power that the prayer attitude has released.

This type of prayer is not something to be crammed down anyone's throat. No one should pray without the impelling desire to fulfill a recognized inner need that cannot be met through any other process than prayer.

In a world suffering from disillusionment and from the ills of spirit and flesh that grow from the denial of the essentially spiritual nature of man, we would open again the doors to the life that was intended for his creatures. We would make to the Master of Life the request his disciples made, "Lord, teach us to pray." And in so praying, we best learn to live.

This type of prayer is the response to an invitation, not made by man, but built into the very core of being. Through it man responds to the highest and deepest within himself, and in that response moves on to the place where he achieves his full stature as a creature, known and loved and fulfilled through an intimate relationship with his Creator.

PART FIVE

The Techniques of Prayer

❧❦❧

26. PRAYER AS QUIET LISTENING

OUR consideration of the techniques of prayer will have little to do with postures, times, and words. Rather it will consider that deeper level of considered activity which brings together the processes of prayer, the disciplines of prayer, and seeks to find the ways they can be employed to bring the praying self to his highest form of spiritual efficiency. To that end we would first consider the importance of the technical mastery of silent listening.

The Scriptures often refer to the significance of silence. "The Lord is in his holy temple, let all the earth keep silence before him." "In quietness and in confidence shall be your strength." It takes a special kind of inner strength to use silence creatively.

At the beginning we must face the fact that we live in the noisiest era in history. We are seldom in silence. Radio, television, or hi-fi is usually turned on. Our cities have alarmingly high decibel rates, and the roar of jet planes reaches remote corners of the land. Amidst such a cacophony of sound, it is difficult to be silent and practice the arts of quietness. Even in group experience we exhibit a selfishness that grows from thinking that our special noise is better than other noises. One evening when a group of friends were at dinner I plugged in the tape recorder without their knowledge and recorded the pleasant conversation that was taking place. After an hour I asked if anyone would like to hear the tape played back. After some initial embarrassment it was heard, and the significant revelation was not in what had been said but the simple fact that seldom had anyone finished a sentence before he was interrupted. It was as if each person felt he knew in advance what the other would say and so did not need to listen. Or perhaps it was that each person felt that what he had to say was so important that it could not wait on the words of another. We are neither used to silence, nor are we usually good listeners, so we have to work harder to become wise users of silence and creative listeners to the communications of others.

The ability to keep silent when another person is speaking demonstrates more than good upbringing. It shows that we accept the other person. Here is the recognition of an opportunity in human relationships where through creative listening one person may accord honor to the other and be enriched by the full quality of the relationship.

The simple meaning of quiet listening is found when one asks a question and genuinely awaits an answer. Too often our questions are rhetorical. We do not really expect answers. The prayer that seeks to communicate without listening is less than half a prayer.

When one listens quietly for an answer he employs empathy, sympathy, and identity. Empathy is the ability to feel with others, to share their emotions. Sympathy is the process of accepting the feelings of others, whether they are good or bad. It recognizes the right of the other to be himself, and to be acceptable as that self. Identity is achieved when the person who asks and the person who answers become one in the moment of true understanding.

Often the asking of the right question is more important than getting the desired answer. There may be no clear and simple answer, but the asking of the question starts mind and emotion at work toward the understanding of the heart of the problem. The quiet stance turns the thinking and feeling process back upon the self, and this stimulates growth.

When Jesus stood accused before Pilate he made no defense

but kept his silence. Pilate in his arrogance thought he was wisely representing the power of the Roman Empire. Jesus looked at him with a silence that showed a depth of understanding and a recognition of the weakness of his vaunted power. Pilate became uneasy when he saw this temporal power had no influence upon this man with his spiritual adequacy. In despair Pilate made threats and then tried to escape his responsibility for what happened to this man who could not be frightened. How could silence be more profound and commanding?

Dostoevski gives classic literary expression to the power of the commanding silence. In the scene with Jesus before the Grand Inquisitor we see the inability of earthly and ecclesiastical authority to cope with the competent spirit. Jesus had been walking the streets of Seville teaching and healing those who came to him, without authorization of the Church. As a result he was called before the Inquisition and accused of using the power of God without the approval of the Church. Jesus stood quietly, and the more he was accused the more guilty became the accuser. Nothing could touch or intimidate the spirit that walked with God. While the Cardinal had the authority of the Church to condemn, he could not condemn what was so much better than himself. He was overwhelmed by his own inadequacy, and in fear threatened death, only to have Jesus kiss his bloodless lips and disappear.

The deep silence of prayer does much the same thing. We move beyond the blusterings of our own superficial adequacy and stand before the presence of the Master who does not accuse or answer back in defensiveness, but lets us measure ourselves by the self he shows could be. Here before the most patient and understanding of all listeners we hear ourselves, we see ourselves, and we pass the clear judgments upon ourselves. The Psalmist knew this experience. "O Lord, thou hast searched me and known me." "Search me and know my heart, try me and know my thoughts and see if there be any wicked way in me, and lead me in the way everlasting." Here one sees identification with God as the creative listener. Saint Theresa of Avila knew the experience of quiet listening and some of the frustration that goes with it. She said, "Do you think he is silent when we do not hear him? He speaks plainly to the heart when we listen to him with the heart."

How often our talking is an effort at escape from having to listen. The discourtesy of a person who monopolizes conversation is quickly noted, but the breakdown of the creature-Creator relationship that comes from the prayer where one merely talks is most tragic. To ask God the questions and then not to wait quietly for the still, small voice that may be giving important answers is not only arrogant but discourteous and unintelligent.

But listening prayer, aware of inner need and willing to lay aside the defenses of much talking and the arrogance that perpetually asks and does not wait for answers, opens up the inner recesses of being so that from the deep silences we can become aware of ourselves, our inner kingdom, and the stirrings of God's spirit within, waiting to be heard and heeded.

The technique of quiet listening is not learned easily for we are inclined to be noisy people. We like nothing better than the sound of our own voices. The practice of quiet listening slowly makes us aware of the fact that we are never spiritually alone, but that a creative conversation can take place within the depths of being as deep speaks unto deep.

Creativity usually springs from quietness. We cannot hear a tree grow, yet the power of God is at work there. The growth of a spirit is not a noisy process, but it can be fostered by the preparation of a self that knows how to listen and is ready and willing to do it.

Jesus urged upon his followers the techniques of quiet listening. He urged them to seek out a quiet place, where they might hear rather than be heard. He made it clear that God knows all our needs without having to be told, but that the important communication takes place when we are prepared to listen. Jesus illustrated this quiet listening in his ministry. He used words sparingly and with the wisdom of one who had learned to listen much and say only what was necessary.

As the Society of Friends has so well illustrated, it is in the depths of silence that the spirit is heard and moves through the lives of men.

27. PRAYER WITHOUT WORDS

WE live in a word-dependent culture. Our lives are continually bombarded by words—the printed word, the spoken word, and those we read between the lines of life's experience. We are educated with words, admonished by words, inspired through words. We can easily be deluded into thinking that words are the ultimate reality.

We need to caution ourselves that words are only symbols. They are not the reality. They stand as proxies for the reality. They sponsor the image or reality. They are the necessary symbols people use to communicate realities.

The usefulness of words as symbols that communicate reality is compromised if we permit words to have highly personalized meanings that vary from person to person. If we are to communicate realities, we must recognize the need to understand precisely what it is that words signify.

Words become whimsical when they encourage the subtle substitution of the secondary for the primary, the make-believe for the real. How readily we employ words when action is needed. How often when faced with the responsibility to act, we formulate and pass a resolution to serve as our surrogate. We even say in parliamentary processes that we have "acted on" a motion when we have merely said "Yea" or "Nay."

Words are substituted for experience, and our chitchat about religious experience is often accorded a stature equal to the actual experience. Words can deteriorate to the status of empty symbols when they obstruct the human experience they are meant to symbolize. So it is easier to say "love" than to be loving. It is easier to explain justice than to act justly. It is simpler to repeat the formulas of belief than to live out the demands that faith puts upon us. Scripture cautions us about words and alerts us to the danger of confusing symbols and realities. The hazard is not so much in the words that are spoken as it is in the way words replace positive action. We talk a good line—period. The unruly member referred to by Saint James is the chatterbox who allows the sound and the fury to obscure the thought and the reason.

How can we in our word-transmitted and word-dependent culture learn to free ourselves of the hazards of words? How can we learn to move beyond the thought-crippling overindulgence in words? How can we learn the discipline of a communication that moves beyond words? How can we guarantee that thought will be the master of its verbal instruments rather than slave to them? It is here that one of the more important contributions of prayer can be made.

Perhaps we can begin by trying to understand the important types of nonverbal communication. A moment of thought will bring to mind a number of incidents where rich and meaningful communication took place at the nonverbal level. Consider the wagging tail of a dog, the purr of a cat, the rustle of leaves, or the look of anxiety on a child's face. No word has been spoken, yet much has been revealed, and we react to the unspoken language that is at work all around us.

Parents soon become sensitive to the range of meaning implicit in their infant's cry. They quickly learn to distinguish between the cry of pain, that of hunger, and that of the urge for attention and play. Each of these types of crying has its special meaning and is immediately understood for what it is —quite different from the cry of fear, anger, or anxiety. Although no words are used, the parent knows the meaning and responds accordingly.

When we stop to think of it, we realize that much important communication is nonverbal. When you know a person well, his facial expressions and gestures say much. The communication is so basic and direct that words seem to be unnecessary. Words are a later development in life and culture, and, while they are most useful in many situations, we are fortunately not entirely dependent upon symbols that are substitutes for the real thing.

Much basic language is continually in use. Beethoven and Bach did not speak English, but we have never let that fact stand in the way of our understanding and appreciation of their musical message. It was never word-dependent. In fact, words could not really add to the language of the musician. An inquisitive student approached a pianist who had just played a Beethoven sonata and said, "Could you please explain it to me?" The pianist stammered for a few moments, failed to find words, and then sat down at the piano and played the sonata again. At the conclusion he asked, "Now do you see?" There are times when the feeling and the meaning are greater than the words we have available to communicate them, and it would diminish the true meaning to try to fit them to inadequate verbal symbols.

I walked through the Wanamaker art gallery one day with

a German artist who had been driven from Germany by Nazi prejudice. Some of his paintings were on display, but he walked through the gallery unknown with a group of interested spectators who were listening to the guide's comments about the pictures. When the lecture was finished I asked the artist what he felt about the commentary on his works of art. In his crisp, limited English he said, "He does not know. I cannot tell." Great experience is always seeking a more authentic means of expression than mere verbal forms, no matter how skillfully they may be used.

It was this higher type of communication that Jesus often used. For him words were a starting point and not a conclusion. He did not use words in place of action, but rather as motivations to action. He painted word pictures that embraced the lives of real people and plausible experiences. His parables were activated and activating words. His words led to choice, decision, and action. "Go and do thou likewise." So also his prayer was a prelude to action, a way of life and not a ritualized use of secondary symbols.

People approached Jesus as if they were aware of something more important than the words he spoke. The woman who touched the hem of his garment was acting out the mood of prayer. She was aware of her need, her illness, and she reached out toward a source of wholeness. She longed for health and did more than say a prayer—she acted her prayer and touched a source of spiritual power. No words were needed, or could they have been an adequate substitute.

Jesus himself was a living example of the struggle for the ultimately real in place of the symbols that can usurp the place of the actual experience. He sought a quiet place for prayer. Quite obviously it was not formal or verbal prayer. It was the prayer that moved beyond words and breviaries to the primal awareness of God in the wonder, mystery, and power of creative love in action. Because he was aware of that dimension of life and sought it diligently, he was able to employ it actively. His perpetual adequacy was living evidence of the fact that he dealt directly with ultimate reality rather than substitutes.

Jesus communicated best with his disciples during moments when spiritual awareness became a primary fact, not an echo. In moments of illumination such as the Mount of Transfiguration, they saw meanings beyond mere facts, they felt emotions beyond mere sensation. They were able to extend the boundaries of being through wordless prayer that awakened sensitivities unlimited by space, time, and power.

These have been the experiences of Paul, who was struck dumb; of Pascal, who for two hours was caught up in wordless wonder that transformed his life; of Thomas Kelly, who found a revelation that came through wordless contemplation. Prayer that is restricted to words pauses at the threshold but may never enter the sanctum sanctorum of true insight.

What can this mean for us? Too often we have been taught to pray in words and do not know that the ultimate of spiritual communication is achieved when the language of the spirit, uncluttered and unencumbered, moves freely to view the meanings that cannot be forced into formal symbols. The use of words with their conventional meanings often drags us back to selfish considerations, mundane relationships, and trivial preoccupations. The prayer that stands in awe before the uncontaminated pictures of spiritual significance may well be a higher form of the discipline of prayer. A physician, devout in prayer and skilled in surgery, told me that he prayed before each operation, not in words, but in a picturing of the figure of Christ as the epitome of healing power, standing beside him to direct his every movement.

Prayer freed of words is a disciplined achievement of focused spiritual energy. It is not easily done. But when it can be accomplished it opens yet another door into the sacred precincts of prayer, and makes it possible for the praying creature to see more clearly toward that divine nature continually revealing itself to man when he is made sensitive by his determined and disciplined effort. Then prayer is not so much a matter of our asking, our words, but of God's revealing, his language speaking powerfully though quietly.

28. PRAYER AS A FINE ART

WE all know something of the nature of art, but few outside the ranks of the artists have any idea of the struggle, the concentration, the effort, and discipline that go into the finished work of power and beauty.

We know that fine art does not just happen. It is carefully cultivated. It is painstakingly done. The medieval phrase "he is a very painful artist" expresses something of the travail innate in the creative process. We still use a phrase that echoes the ancient idea when we say, "He is taking great pains with his work." The discipline of the spirit incident to great creative effort is always accomplished as the end result of strenuous acts and accepted suffering. Although there is something in all of us that resists the bonds of such discipline, there is also something else that can see goals and accept the obligations of the discipleship necessary to attain the goals.

We readily concede that the budding concert pianist cannot casually walk past a piano once or twice a day and strike a few random notes and achieve his purpose. Nor can the apprentice sculptor take an occasional whack at the marble with his chisel and expect to see a work of art emerge. The way of the artist requires devotion, singleness of purpose, diligent study of himself and others, and unending practice that is ruthless in its self-criticism.

Any fine art is the perfect blending of a significant idea, an adequate medium, a disciplined person, and competent relation of the three elements. Prayer as a supreme art of the human spirit is no exception to these rules.

Prayer aims to bring fullest realization to the total being. Prayer adds something to life that was not there before. This added quality is more than the fulfillment of something unrealized within man's human nature, though that may well be a part of it. It is more than the use of the adequate self in spiritual communication, though, to be sure, it includes that. It is essentially the self come alive with new power and new possibility not explained by anything within the range of man's understanding of himself and his life. When this is realized and observed by the praying individual it is not easily denied, though it is in a category of experience all its own. It stretches the medium of human awareness, but it does not create the grotesque in doing so. Rather, it reveals the most sublime response to life.

When Madame Curie stood before a little receptacle that glowed with radioactive substance, she shared a magnificent but awesome moment. She saw before her an element that broke the molds of all organized human thought in the world of the physical sciences. What previously was declared impossible was now a reality. What was disruptive of all previous belief was clearly revealed to her disciplined consciousness. Nothing that has happened since that night can change the fact of her experience. Yet everything in the world of scientific thought from that moment to this has had to take into account those few milligrams of radium.

The artist is always engaged in creating something new. The master of the fine art of prayer is perpetually engaged in creating newness of life, a richness of human thought that is persistently aware of divine possibilities and purposes. Sometimes the insights that come with creative newness of life are wrenching, searing hand grenades of insight bursting upon life to disrupt old patterns, disfigure old images, and destroy old illusions. The insight of the artist is prepared for this result of creative effort, and he cannot continue to live in the future as if these spiritual powers had not been let loose in life. The discoverer of new elements of the spirit can be no less sensitive to new powers let loose in life than the creative thinker can be in the field of science. In his insight into the meaning and power of prayer Jesus discovered a new element in man's nature. We cannot exist as if his discovery had not been made.

Prayer as a fine art always involves a great idea, a responsive medium, and the disciplined spirit of the venturesome being. Our day of dependence upon things material and an interest in control of external things may be ill-prepared to consider this mastery of the inner being, but surely we need to rediscover this lost art. When we lose something we are wise to begin the search where we saw it last. We could not do better than looking at the life of Jesus where this lost art was realized in its finest form. Jesus found meaning and power for life in the attitude of prayer. What was the idea, the medium, and the discipline for him?

With Jesus the great idea was the capacity for God-consciousness in the soul of man. When this idea was let loose in life man could not direct his face toward the earthly roots of his physical nature, but rather must look toward that revelation of life's meaning that is found in his special endowment. Thus the creatively sensitive soul moves beyond the boundaries that the mind would ordinarily set up for its efforts at communication. Man then relates himself directly with the nature of God in the quest for divine self-revelation at once sublime and also ultimately real. In this process, and perhaps only here, the human spirit rises to its full stature, and asserts its claim to that sonship—the creature made in the image of God. This assertion is never made in arrogance. Rather, it is the ultimate submission of the humble soul that knows its mastery of expression is achieved only as one learns to bear the full meaning of the terrifying burden of God-consciousness.

The medium for this responsiveness through prayer is the raw material of life itself—the human experience: the daily use of time and space, of thought and feeling, of self-awareness, the awareness of others, and the awareness of God in relation to all that happens to the experiencing being. Jesus in living the human existence showed how the daily experience could be used to bring the human and divine into active, creative relationship.

Through the effort to make the human will completely compatible with the divine will, Jesus revealed how the mastery of the great idea and the creative use of the medium could bring its full realization in the disciplined human spirit. Only as the spirit of man was determined to fulfill to its utmost its relationship to God was the sublime possibility of human life brought to its most artful expression. Here, then, the art of living found its transcendent creative actualization.

The sciences of life verify the possibility of such a capacity for transcendence. Some human experience cannot be understood apart from such verification. But the creative act does not depend upon its verification, for it has its own validity. The truly creative always has something about it that is beyond the propositions of logic. It is the nature of high religion to reveal it in experience, but even here the task of religious consciousness is to lead the person to the place where it is possible for him to participate in the experience; it is not to furnish the experience itself. One can train the artist to use his medium and discipline himself in relation to it, but the creative act is so intensely personal that it must be the projection of something deep within the self that transcends the self in the very act of becoming.

Beethoven's *Fifth Symphony* is something more than the meeting of the mind of the composer with the idea of that composition. In the meeting a new quality is added. The sheer barbarism of some of its musical passages and the sublimely courageous theme of the whole carry with them and transmit to others the transcendent meaning of the soul that is responding to its creative potential. It then becomes a language of its own, but it speaks only to those who have prepared themselves to listen.

So it is that the unfamiliar spiritual quality can possess life and transform it. For even though we cannot explain, we can experience. It is unscientific to deny the experience that is a part of life. The processes of prayer, then, while they do not deny the scientific, fulfill a deeper level of our existence, and are more nearly comparable to the venture of the artist. We do not understand the full meaning of prayer unless we approach it as an artist. We do not realize its full meaning for life until we grasp the use of prayer as employed in the life of that great artist of living, the quiet man of Galilee who demonstrated the art in its finest form.

29. THE TECHNIQUES OF PRAYER

WE live in an age that is concerned with techniques, the how of doing things. We feel that if we can master the technical aspects of any process we are well on the road to success.

While it is true that technique is important with external processes, we mislead ourselves if we conclude that a safe and sure set of rules exists that can guarantee our mastery of the art of prayer. The skills of the inner life are not so much concerned with the "How" as they are with the "Why." Yet we cannot consider the art of prayerful living and completely ignore the matters related to techniques and skills appropriate in the life of prayer.

It is important for us to realize at the beginning that our approach to prayerful activity will be concerned not so much with externals as internals. Too often we have been led to believe that prayer involves fixed principles of posture, place, and procedure. Our concern is more with something far more basic than that. Nevertheless, preparation for prayer, engaging the total being in prayer, and fulfilling the obligations of prayer do invite our consideration of skills and self-discipline.

Any venture as important as prayer should be planned with great care. In an earlier chapter we spoke of the importance of relaxation. Now we should speak of the conditioning of the mind and spirit through anticipation, the preparation of the whole being by exercising the belief. This may be achieved by strengthening one's faith by examining the power of faith at work in the lives of others. The reading of great devotional classics provides one way of doing this. There is an abundance of devotional literature on the insights and experiences of great men and women of prayer who have lived in the past. This rich literature of the spirit makes a good launching pad for the soaring mind and emotion.

Often the tempo of life moves so rapidly that it takes some time to wait quietly to deescalate to the point where mind and spirit are adjusted to the processes that cannot be hurried. In this way the emerging object of concentration is brought into a clear vision and the object of prayer is winnowed out from the myriad thoughts and feelings that are normally predominant.

Jesus demonstrated the importance of proper preparation for prayer by withdrawing to quiet places alone. Here in solitude he could anticipate, meditate, and concentrate. In this way he set the stage for the important communication that prayer can provide.

If we are to entertain an important guest, we look forward to the event with expectancy. We make sure that the house is spotless, the larder filled, and the other responsibilities of the host adequately met. If we would prepare for an earthly guest so carefully, how much more important it is for us to do all that is possible within ourselves to "make straight the way for the Lord."

After proper preparation, the next step is the engaging of the total being in prayer. This calls for bringing the being of God and the being of the man at prayer into a demanding and a fulfilling relationship.

In an athletic contest there are long periods of preparation for that moment when we put our very best effort into the specialized action. The whole being is refined to the most perfect condition so that in the contest the coordination, the skill, and the performance can register the peak of our performance.

Prayer brings the athlete of the spirit to the place where he makes equally strenuous demands upon his total being. He seeks to be ready to enter into the most exacting relationship that he as a human can achieve. In order to gain the fruits of that relationship, he first expresses the thankfulness he feels at being able to engage in such rewarding communication. His ability to be thankful brings the picture of life into a realistic balance. To come into this relationship without a full awareness of the privilege of the relationship undermines its possibility for fulfillment.

In addition to thanksgiving there is also the need for a commanding sense of the wonder, power, truth, and goodness of God. This invites the inner response of praise.

Then comes the demand for honest self-examination to measure clearly success and failure. This complete honesty is the basis for self-change, and it is one of the remarkable achievements of prayer. We have an amazing built-in ability to justify, rationalize, and excuse the self. We need complete candor and frank self-judgment to make the creature-Creator encounter productive of change.

Having faced ourselves honestly and measured our human state with the divine demands upon our living, we are impelled toward dedication and commitment. This is the time for resolve and the redirection of energy on the basis of the honest measurement of ourselves in the mirror of divine expectation. We must sweep away the self-justification, the petty indulgences, the corroding angers and stand exposed before our spiritual goal.

When this is done we are in a position to move into the larger and better self. This self then is prepared to engage in the demanding act of prayer for others, not in verbal rehearsal but in using the total resources of our being to mediate the healing, redeeming love of God that can be manifest through us.

When we become this living expression of loving concern, we are prepared to move on from the total engaging of the being in prayer to the final stage of fulfilling the obligations of our praying. This is the most demanding discipline of all, for now we are expecting ourselves to act, think, feel, and live as we have prayed.

What do we do when we finish praying? It is a misconception to think that we ever finish our prayer. If we have really been praying with the whole being, we dedicate ourselves to a way of life that implements in action the revelations that come to us in the spiritual encounter with our divine spiritual counterpart. The self that is continually being modified, purified, and molded by the processes of prayer finds its verification in the way of life that activates the insights of contemplation, meditation, and communion that have been achieved.

Too often when we are faced with the demands of this kind of prayer we seek to escape from it. The ways of God that would be revealed through us are too much for our frail natures to accept. We are tempted to say that we do not have time for this kind of prayer. The excuse offered is that we might become too religious if we acted as if God were continually at work in and through us. Whatever the efforts at escape may be, we do not really deceive ourselves, for we know that time can be found when we deem the cause to be really important.

The choice of what is important in living is ours to make. We might begin by setting aside a block of time each day to practice the techniques of prayer. While no one way is satisfactory for everyone, the following procedure may help to introduce you to the kind of prayer we have been talking about. Reserve a half hour each morning and evening. Divide this period into ten minutes for preparation, ten minutes for projecting the mind in creative, wholesome thought about life and its meaning, and ten minutes more for self-examination and plans for the realization of the goals of life contemplated in prayer. Such deliberate effort to move into the antechambers of spiritual communication will help to break through the veil of unknowing that separates our human nature from its divine counterpart. With practice, the concern for minutes and time will be replaced by an increased awareness of the presence of God. Then you will know increasingly what the mystics meant when they spoke of "practicing the presence of God." The artist may discipline himself for technical mastery, but he achieves his greatness when the technique is swallowed up in the realization of creative power. The fulfillment of the technical mastery of prayer comes when technique is no longer a concern, but the awareness of the presence of God so fills the consciousness that the self is lost in its fullest self-realization.

This then is the kind of experience that can change life. Prayer is the heart and soul of the religious experience. It is the point where the disciplined, mastered self finds the barriers that may exist between creature and Creator evaporating before that divine encounter that is the goal and end of man, the act of standing fulfilled in the relationship with God that lifts the capacity for God-consciousness to its full realization.

30. THE ATTITUDES OF PRAYER

WE know that a proper attitude toward any project is an ingredient important to success. One's mood surely can modify the state of his being. All other things being equal, the mood and attitude the person brings to his task becomes a contributive factor in its fulfillment. This is certainly true of prayer.

How did Jesus approach the process of prayer? First of all, he believed totally in the efficacy of prayer. He believed that in prayer we align ourselves with infinite power and wisdom. In prayer we are fulfilled because we become one with God. In prayer our potential as spiritual beings is realized because we yield to God that his will may be made known in and through us. The mind of Christ was a believing mind. We gain insight into the proper attitude toward prayer by looking at the quality of his mind at prayer.

Not even in the solitude of prayer did Jesus feel lonely.

At all times he felt the unfailing presence of God. Even in the hour of bitterest suffering he was not afraid to direct his cry of despair as a prayer, "My God, why hast thou forsaken me?" He felt the unfailing privilege and opportunity of approach to God. He was continually aware of the universal mind of God that was actively seeking him as he sought it. For Jesus, prayer was never a venture into the unknown. It was a rendezvous where the finite and infinite met. We too can believe that in prayer we are never alone, but are standing at the point where creature and Creator become one in integral unity.

A further point concerns the attitude of openness that is essential to prayer. How often we approach life and new experiences with closed minds. Our science-oriented minds erect restrictive barriers around contemplation and God-directed thoughts. Obeisance is shown to past observations, and only that which can be measured and recorded is considered to be important. Such glorification in natural law overlooks the romance of the greatest breakthroughs in the history of science. There are facts that are beyond known law, and these are the yet unprobed new and larger laws waiting to be encountered and formulated. In the personal life of man this is more readily demonstrated to be true. In the process of prayer there is no place for a closed universe or a closed mind.

Any traveler in need of directions must be able to ask the right questions. By asking the wrong questions, one can hardly expect to get the right answers. A blocked or closed mind can confront God and be completely unaware of the divine presence. Jesus was unable to perform mighty works only at times when people asked the wrong questions. "Isn't this Joseph the carpenter's son?" Because they could not ask the right questions they could not get the right answers. They drew curtains down around their minds and shut out the light that could have erased their darkness. They thought they knew all of the answers to the irrelevant questions they asked, and that ended things for them. They shut the door to Jesus. There is nothing more destructive of the mood of prayer than a closed mind, one that thinks it knows all of the answers before a single question is asked.

Another attitude commended by Jesus was man's hunger and thirst for righteousness. Or as the poet says it,

Like tides on a crescent sea beach,
    When the moon is new and thin,
Into our hearts high yearnings
    Come welling and surging in;
Come from this mystic ocean
    Whose rim no foot has trod.
Some of us call it longing,
    And others call it God.[1]

This longing for God stirs the whole being like an insatiable appetite that hungers for the bread of life, and the living waters from springs that never fail. This openness of spirit is basic and essential to the beginning and end of prayer.

One more prerequisite is the capacity for expectancy. How often people approach prayer without the slightest expectation of a response. They say in effect, "I am praying, but I know nothing is going to happen." I remember the shock I received once when summoned to the bedside of one of my parishioners. The wife met me at the door and tearfully urged me to pray for her husband. When I came downstairs again she followed me to the door and said. "While you are here I might as well talk with you about plans for the funeral." Either this woman was abysmally ignorant of the power of prayer, or she was practicing an all too prevalent blasphemy. To engage in prayer and at the same time deny its efficacy is an inversion of faith. It is expectancy in reverse.

[1] William Herbert Carruth, "Each in His Own Tongue."

The Scriptures speak to us clearly about expectancy as an attitude of prayer. Here it is pointed out that it was done to them according as they expected. Expectancy is a barometer of faith. If we are conflicted in our faith we cannot help but be handicapped in the outcome of our praying.

Openness and expectancy lead directly to the capacity to respond. We begin to function at a higher level of being when we surrender ourselves wholly to the will of God in full confidence that this will is the supreme law of the universe.

We do not easily surrender all of our petty thoughts. We impose limits on God. We say we will believe in God and practice the disciplines of prayer if everything comes out the way we want it. But prayer is a matter of total self-surrender. The art of letting go must be mastered. We cannot force prayer into our mold and expect the will of God to be made manifest. Our responsiveness must be like shifting into a spiritual overdrive where we move beyond the conflicts of interest that grow from trying to impose our wills upon the universe. Prayer finally leads man to surrender his willfulness, false pride, and limiting judgments so that he may be completely responsive to God's will, even though this may involve a cross.

Robert G. Ingersoll was an influential lecturer, a popular philosopher, and an agnostic. He invaded the minds of many persons with his questioning of faith and assertions that gullible people believed too much for their own good. He said that if people could really see Jesus as he was, stripped of the adulation of praise of the centuries, he would no longer be worshiped. He urged his friend, the novelist Lew Wallace, to write a book about the Jesus that really was. Wallace went to work to expose Jesus for what he was, a man among men. In the effort to acquire an accurate background for his book he had to study the New Testament, become acquainted with the events of the life of Jesus, and evaluate the impact of those events upon the people of his day. The more he studied the life and ministry of Jesus, the more he realized he was no ordinary man. When he came face to face with the man that was, he was overcome with awe, and became a worshiper. The book intended to put an end to the superficial worship of Jesus led the author to a profound revelation of the unique being who found God in the communion of spirit that true prayer employs. In the life of Jesus, Wallace found a depth of meaning, of openness, of expectant faith, and sublime action that overwhelmed him with new spiritual insight.

We risk the practice of idolatry in our worship whenever we dwell on the superficial, manmade forms of worship. But, when we stand quietly before the Master of Prayer we gain new depths of understanding that change life. Jesus never asked to be worshiped, but he did ask us to follow in the adventure of prayerful living that could open the frontiers of being to the full meaning of God consciousness.

Someone has said that God's good news is simply that we are invited to meet him through Jesus, the Christ. When we experience that divine encounter we realize that prayer is not something we do. Rather, it is something that happens to us. It becomes a realization of true being, of spiritual becoming. It opens the doors of life to the meaning God intended life to have for us, and then the King of Glory can come in.

31. THE GROUP PROCESS IN PRAYER

THE recent decade has seen a great new development of small-group prayer activity. Hundreds of people are praying together in closely knit fellowship of spiritual adventure and are finding new measurements for life and new experience in spiritual comradeship.

This is a recapturing of the way of life of the early church. In the first century, the Christians had no church buildings, no well-developed organization, no professionally trained leadership. They met together in homes, fields, even in catacombs. The very nature of the organized life of the early church demanded that it practice the arts of small-group action. It was this movement of small bands of powerfully motivated people that changed the Roman Empire and finally controlled it. However, with ecclesiastical and political power, something significant was lost. Perhaps most significant was the loss of the spiritually valid experience of those who practiced the fellowship of spiritual exploration and adventure.

Wherever the church in history has been spiritually vigorous there has been small-group prayer activity taking place. The monastic orders separated themselves from the world to do works of the spirit and practical works for humanity. The dedication to the life of prayer among the Franciscans and the Augustinians, for instance, contributed to major changes within the life of the church, both Protestant and Roman Catholic.

John Wesley recognized the importance of small-group action for the vitality of the Wesleyan revival. With a keen understanding of group dynamics, he used three different group formations for different purposes. The prayer bands were limited to seven or eight members and met for the purpose of self-examination and discipline in the spiritual life. The class meetings were primarily for the study of the Bible and spiritual classics and in size were limited to twelve or fifteen. The societies were made up of the combined bands and class meetings and were brought together primarily for worship and the support of the overall group life. Modern study of group procedure attests the wisdom of Wesley both as to the group purpose and the size best suited to achieving the purpose.

The Society of Friends with its emphasis on the life of the spirit and quiet prayer also has employed the small-group process. The power of the Quaker movement both in social reform and in the development of the disciplines of the spirit has been out of proportion to its numerical strength, and affirms again the power of a small-group, prayer-centered program in action.

The modern movement within the church to recapture the mood of the early church has found a significant instrument in the small-group process, for there are powers released in group action that tend to multiply the individual's strength and purpose.

The small group recaptures many of the strong emotional relationships that develop within the family. The close bonds of feeling and communication make it possible for persons to break through the restraints they usually feel and recognize and express their deeper feelings and aspirations with freedom and satisfaction. The praying group achieves a comradeship and intimacy at the level of life's deeper meaning that brings stimulus to the growth of the spirit. The friendly, accepting atmosphere reduces fears and apprehensions and releases confidence and the type of good will that furthers spiritual sensitivity.

As we mentioned earlier, there seems to be something about the stimulus of group action that gives energy to the Holy Spirit. In the records of the New Testament church there is no instance recorded when the Holy Spirit came upon an individual. Always it was a kindling process that came about when two or three or more persons were gathered together with a common mind. Something important was let loose in the life of the group that did not exist explicitly in the life of the individuals who made it up.

The praying group is a growing group, not in numerical size primarily, but in the spiritual perception of its individual members. The very nature of this growth produces interchange of thought and feeling so that the members find further stimulation for growth. The individual becomes increasingly aware of his meaning and value as a spiritual being, and life itself becomes more significant for him as he lives it with sensitivity to its spiritual meaning and purpose.

The small group at prayer is emotionally supportive of its members. Even though most of the praying be done in silence, the shared mood and common goals make each member feel secure in the spiritual quest that he is engaged in. As one person stated it, "I feel more myself in a prayer group than anywhere else in life."

There is also a psychic energy that can be let loose in a closely knit group which operates with singleness of purpose. We have a growing understanding of those qualities of the human mind that engage in effective communication beyond language and ordinary sensory processes. This extrasensory capacity seems to be cultivated in the mood and atmosphere of prayer and spiritual exercise. It may well be that this psychic energy is magnified in a group process so that not only is the Holy Spirit more likely to be present, but also the works of the spirit may be more adequately performed.

The burden of self-consciousness tends increasingly to separate persons from fruitful communication as the consciousness of self increases. But the subjection of self-consciousness to God-consciousness breaks through the walls of separation and makes it possible for persons in the praying group to be most completely together without violating the awareness of self that is basic to any fruitful communication. This, then, makes the group at prayer the family-sized equivalent of the redemptive community.

The modern church with its complex of buildings and its round-the-clock program of activities may well make it seem that spiritual activity is a specialized function for specially trained persons. A member may hear the pastor pray and the choir sing and feel that in the midst of all of this skilled activity there is little place for his amateur participation. This mood is unfortunate, and, as long as it exists, the church violates its true nature. There are no amateur spirits made in the image of God, as the principle of the priesthood of all believers makes clear. Any practice that obscures or limits man's awareness of his spiritual nature is unfortunate. Any act or process that makes men increasingly aware of their true natures as spiritual beings serves the ultimate purpose for which the church exists.

The modern mood makes it easy for persons to be spectators rather than participators. When it comes to the development of his own unique spiritual nature, no growth takes place at the spectator's pew. Only those who enter the struggle for values and exercise their spirits as participators can share the fulfillment that is essential to spiritual realization.

So in this day and age more than in some other eras there is a need for the shared experience that stimulates growth of the spirit. In the midst of church programs that favor bigness and statistical measurements, the salvation of the church may be found in the small groups that are comfortable with their smallness because it makes it possible to be aware of the spiritually unique nature of its individual member.

A church I know, near the heart of a great city, was influenced by the values of the city. In some respects the church was like a country club, sponsoring interesting programs, giving status to its members, and practicing an elite type of discrimination that made those of other strata of society feel so unwelcome that they quietly disappeared. Into this church came a few persons with an interest in transforming its values to bring them more into conformity with the New Testament ideal. At first, a prayer group was formed to encourage spiritual discovery. After a year or so it had grown to the place where it was divided into two groups. Within a few years there were several groups practicing their quiet disciplines in such a way that the whole church had been profoundly changed. It worked toward new goals, valued people for different reasons, and practiced the privileges of an international, interracial, and interdenominational fellowship. To be sure, there were some hazards, for the small groups tended to become a church within a church, and might have begun to feel that they were superior beings. But the hazard was honestly faced and adequate compensation made. The important thing that happened was that sincerely dedicated persons' lives could be transformed through a disciplined spiritual life that was shared through the small-group process. As a by-product the life of a church was remade so that a distinguished visitor who came to live in it and study it as an interesting phenomenon in adult education left with the comment, "This is the nearest thing to a New Testament church I have ever seen. I wouldn't have believed it if I hadn't seen it."

Through the action and interaction of persons in small groups, there had developed a new awareness of and respect for the spiritual meaning of life. This had made it easier to value and respect the spiritual potential of others without regard for the superficial judgments so often passed. This respect for self and others made it possible to quietly remake the values of the church and find a new and closer walk with God as a living presence dwelling in an inner kingdom now discovered for the first time.

32. LEARNING TO PRAY FOR OTHERS

❦

IT has long been a practice in the church and among the spiritually disciplined to intercede for others through the use of prayer. This type of prayer is a demanding discipline for it employs a faith that would see the other not subject to disease or disturbance but as a whole being. Often great claims are made for this use of prayer, but the very act of making claims seems to be a denial of the humility essential in coming into communication with the Divine Nature to share the great will that has cosmic proportions.

Sometimes the spectacular results that appear to come through prayer for others are baffling because they raise questions of morality and justice that are not easily answered. Why should some be spared and others not, just because of the efficacy of prayer? Are there certain conditions that have to be fulfilled in order for the power of prayer to be operative? If that is the case, why do some of those who have achieved the finest quality of spirit suffer while others have manifestations of the power of prayer that come almost without asking?

Merely asking the questions seems to place them beyond an easy answer. However, there are needs to be fulfilled, though sometimes we ourselves are not sure what they are. We do the best we know to respond to the spiritual power at work within us even though we continue to admit our basic ignorance concerning many of the more important questions we would ask about this power.

Perhaps we have here a clue to what Carl Jung called a collective unconscious that is at work among us. In the communicative fellowship of those who pray and those who respond to prayer, life is redirected and its needs fulfilled. When we watch a flock of thousands of starlings, we witness the response to some collective sense that operates among them. With no apparent signal the course is changed and there are no stragglers. A communication exists that tends to make them one. So the responsiveness to prayer may not be so much an individual act as it is the drawing upon a reservoir of spiritual power that has been created and to which we continue to be responsive.

Communication itself is life-conditioning. Often persons react positively to a sermon and say, "Things have changed since I heard that sermon." But such a sermon is more than words. It is a meeting of minds where a solution for life speaks to a need of life. Such communication is an instrument for instituting and sustaining a divine relationship through which the transcendent may be at work. It doesn't always happen. One person may sleep through a sermon that is saving the soul of another. The amount of special need and the quality of the response are important parts of the communication, for it demands a sensitive receiver as well as a competent sender.

Prayer is a form of extraordinary communication that seems to operate with a selective response. Just as telepathy is not universally operative but works where there are those with a special sensitivity, so the communication of prayer appears to be more effective with some than with others. This is probably demonstrable in the varied responses to intercessory prayer where one mind and soul deliberately seek to bring spiritual power to work in the life of another person who has a recognized need.

Because for many the activity of prayer is most explicit in

the crises of life, the prayer of intercession gives an opportunity to test the praying response. The intercessory prayer seeks the wholeness of another. It works on the premise that God's will for all his creatures is to be made whole and sustained in that wholeness. When the native state of equilibrium and balance is disrupted by willfulness, disease, or ignorance, it becomes an occasion for seeking restored health and wholeness.

All healing is of God. It is the work of the natural processes of the body. When a doctor gives medicine, the medicine does not do the healing. It merely serves to assist the natural restorative forces already existent in the body. So it is said, "The patient is responding," or, "The patient does not respond." When a surgeon uses the scalpel to remove offending tissue, he removes what impedes healthy functioning. In so doing he helps to release the processes of the body to restore health. If that does not happen it can be said, "The operation was a success but the patient died." The healing process is not created by the practitioner. He assists it.

Faith also is a healing agent. Surgeons often refuse to operate on a person in a state of depression, for the attitude of mind may work so actively upon the body chemistry that it threatens the desired healing process. The person who is rooted in faith and approaches the crises of life with calmness and confidence is fortified for what will take place, and his system is aided in its normal functioning by its mental attitude.

The person of faith may be temporarily overwhelmed by his affliction, like the drowning person, and may need a period of spiritual artificial respiration to restore his being to its desired state.

When the followers of Jesus sought his aid for sick friends, they made strenuous efforts to get them into the presence of Jesus, where he could see and touch them. In intercession something similar takes place. The concerned bring before the Creator of Life those whose lives need redeeming and restoring.

Not all prayers are answered in the way that we in our human weakness may desire. We believe we know the will of God. It is made explicit in the Scriptures. However, our finiteness can never be allowed to stand in the way of the infinite. We pray not for success nor for our will, but that we may be used as dedicated beings for the purposes God would encourage. This calls for humanity, love, and expectancy.

We pray not to manipulate the Creator. That would be an inexcusable act of arrogance. We pray to be used to fulfill God's will through a power that is operative from person to person. If we neglect this power we are remiss. If we deny its efficacy we reject the basic tenets of the spiritual tradition we have inherited.

Prayer for wholeness may be the result of group action as well as individual effort. There is a collective strength in the healing fellowship. Much human injury comes through separation and loneliness and much restoration can come through relation, communication, and participation. The group response of joy or sorrow can be contagious. The intercessory group can add a new quality of interrelatedness in the social patterns that too often symbolize competition and mutual destruction.

There is some confusion in our day as to the means of affecting natural forces. We readily accept the methods of the applied sciences. We feel confidence in the methods of research. Why is it that we feel there is something dependable about a row of test tubes in a laboratory and feel uncertain about a man at prayer? Why do we place our confidence in formulas and reject the spiritual potential of the mind who made the formulas? Man is the more complicated and powerful creation. Man gives the scientific method any validity it may have. The mind of man is the creator of the applied sciences. The application of his spiritual insight when applied to the redemption of life cannot be of lesser value.

Faith is the common ingredient in scientific research as well as in the soul's realization through prayer. They may be different manifestations, to be sure, but they emanate from the same reservoir of the soul of man. Both proceed with the mood of expectation. Both assume that proper results can be found when proper conditions are met. Both accept failure, not as a judgment upon man or science, but as a part of the process of growth toward that greater competence that can bring man closer to the revelation of ultimate truth.

When persons came to Jesus, the one quality that he seemed to emphasize for their restoration to wholeness was faith, active and expectant. This positive attitude toward life seemed to be generated by Jesus. His own faith was communicated so that the people who heard him were often changed in noticeable ways. Those who came to him were not deluged with theological jargon. Nor were they exposed to moralizations. Jesus moved to the central attitude toward life and asked, "Would you be made whole?" Do you want the best in life? Are you willing to generate the faith that can make it so?

This method is not in conflict with the details of medical judgment or practice. It functions at a higher level. In effect, so-called faith healing is concerned with the healing of one's faith. The results of a healed faith cannot help but touch all of life, body, mind, and spirit. We get off the track if we become engaged in listing symptoms and prescribing superficial changes in states of being. Our concern is with the basic change of being, the flooding of life with a faith that makes itself known in every facet of life.

This fine art of praying for others may be the most demanding of the forms of prayer, for it demands of us the faith we would see brought to life in those for whom we pray.

PART SIX

The Fruits of Prayerful Living

‰

33. REMAKING OUR PERSONAL HISTORY

❧

EACH of us is continually at work creating his own biography or life story. Those who chronicle the events of life in biography or autobiography usually list the important deeds that involve time and place, actions and reactions. These are the objective facts of life. But behind the things that are worked out in space and time is another important world, one that is not as easily available to the biographer, but which is probably more important. This is the realm of thought and feeling, the inner world of being where the decisions are made that reveal themselves in external events. "For out of the heart come the issues of life."

The most important aspect of anyone's personal history is written in the secret place of his being where no acting or camouflage can shut the person off from his own self-awareness. Behind the things we do there is always the person we are. The realm of inner meanings and personal values is the seedbed in which we germinate the motives and actions that become the objective record of our living, our personal life story.

Often as we look at our accomplishments in life and our feelings about life, we admit failure and recognize that we have fallen short of the good life to which we aspired. This becomes explicit in the life of the externally motivated person who has not reached the external goals he sought. It is also at work in the life of the internally motivated person who feels that his goals and values have not been enough and his days are steeped in frustration and futility. How, then, can these states of being be changed? How can a person go about rewriting his personal history?

If life is to be ultimately measured by its values and meanings, this is the point where reevaluation must begin. Martin Buber suggests that the life that is built around I-it relationships becomes increasingly depersonalized. Its values are essentially materialistic and the creative, human elements of the being atrophy, for they are not brought into use. The self that relates itself primarily to things tends to become more like a thing than a being. On the other hand, Buber says that the life that is enriched by I-Thou relationships moves beyond material considerations to personal values and meanings. The prophetic confrontation is the point where the *I* of the being confronts the *Thou* of creation and wrests from it its personal meaning. For such a person the universe is not a heartless machine grinding on its relentless way, but is rather the living manifestation of great creative power seeking to reveal the meanings incident to the creative process. In a materialistic, competitive culture where money is the gauge of success and values are evolved from thing-consciousness, it is understandable that the quiet yearnings of the inner being may be lost in the maze of spiritual denials that are implicit in so many daily acts. This leaves little to choose from as far as the life of the soul is concerned between the official atheism of Communist states and the practical atheism of a thing-dominated culture.

Where men have become increasingly materialistic in their living, they have lost their spiritual sensitivity. Where the church has been preoccupied with externals, it has tended to lose its spiritual authority. This has been pointed out by Nicolas Berdyaev in his last book, *Truth and Revelation*. "In the nineteenth century liberal Protestant thought passed judgment upon revelation from the point of view of scientific truth."[1]

[1] (New York: Collier Books, 1962), p. 7.

This truth was concerned with externals, measurements, and thing-consciousness. The preoccupation with external measurements produced an atmosphere of doubt about the validity and meaning of internally revealed truth. In fact, the truths of science were substituted for the truth of revelation. This was the source of deceptive security for nineteenth-century man, but made him doubly vulnerable when the twentieth century came with its new concept of things material. Then it was quite obvious that it was unwise to confuse truths with the truth, for truths may change from age to age, but the truth is a cosmically stable phenomenon continually being revealed in lesser or greater amounts to the men who are prepared to receive it.

The spiritually sensitive person, one who practices the disciplines of prayer, may be continually exposing his being to the truth in the midst of the truths. To the degree that he relates the truths to the truth he is able to bring the world of external things under the control of the inner kingdom of spiritual meanings. But should the process of prayer be limited by the restraints upon freedom that the objective world imposes, his very prayer will become the unwilling slave of the material values that crowd in upon life.

The frustrated being, who goes through his days seeking meaning and value in externals, may well discover for himself that his search is fruitless for he is in effect "seeking the living among the dead." Meaning cannot be found amidst the meaningless, and ultimately things have no intrinsic meaning. Their only meaning is given to them by the Being who is capable of creating meaning. The achievement of meaning is essentially a spiritual act. When meaning is found in the inner kingdom of spiritual truth, it then can be attributed to the things of the external world, but the external meanings are always the product of the inner kingdom, and cannot exist in and of themselves. So it is that the materialistic regimes of Communist states are doomed to failure, for they progress with no real meaning. As long as there is a hangover of meaning from the past, they may stagger on into the meaningless future. Or the needs of the soul of man may assert themselves in rejecting the inadequate materialistic philosophy in the name of creative necessity. In Russia, the scientists and artists have already started an assault on dialectical materialism which gives political form to the I-it relationship. In its stead they seek some source of freedom that makes it possible for truth to be found.

As individuals in the Communist state have found it essential to their intellectual life to deny an inadequate philosophy of history, so also the person oppressed by the practical materialism of the Western world must break through the restraints upon his freedom to declare the independence of his creating nature. As Berdyaev puts it:

> Revelation in history has value only insofar as it is a revelation of truth, an encounter with truth, in other words a revelation of the spirit. . . . Truth is the meaning of life, and life must serve its own meaning. . . . The knowledge of truth is attained by the aggregate of the spiritual powers of man and not by his intellectual faculties alone. And this is determined by the fact that truth is spiritual, that it is life and spirit. . . . When it is spiritual it is God revealing himself in knowledge and thought.[2]

Anything less than this idea of truth is enslaving. The creative life demands freedom from the measurement of things. The life of the spirit by its very nature is already a participant in the infinite and eternal.

The fact that man's inner nature is aware of the nature of truth, and yet is continually submerged in the thing-consciousness of daily living, places a demand upon life that it declare

[1] *Ibid.,* pp. 40, 41, 47.

its independence, assert its freedom, and engage in the creative acts and attitudes that are essential to spiritual growth and the grasp of truth. As long as man lives apart from the true spiritual nature, he does not move from potential to actual. He may put off the time when his spiritual nature can assert itself until that spiritual nature, like Kierkegaard's goose, has become fat, lazy, and comfortable with material things, and so cannot soar into the realm of its true being.

Too often the values of life are externally determined, and we are urged to look like, smell like, and act like some public figure who is held up as a symbol of success. Few are the impulses that urge us to be ourselves and find our best self. But only as this inner core of being asserts itself are we on the road toward finding the meaning of our existence. Our day is throwing new light on the meaning of the inner being, the life of the inner kingdom. Now we know that faith is the inner achievement of meaning that gives substance to works.

Twentieth-century man shares in the venturesome exploration of his psychocentric nature. The true meaning of human life is not found in the chronicling of external events, but in the developing of a soul so responsive to truth that it is continually giving spiritual meaning to the external events.

Each of us, then, is continually engaged in writing his own personal history. It becomes a real history of the person, however, when it is motivated by spiritual creativity. At no point in experience does man come face to face with this aspect of his being more completely than when he accepts the disciplines of prayer and seeks the fruits of prayerful living. Prayer is the process that develops the sensitivity of the inner kingdom, relates it to its ultimate cosmic meaning, and fulfills that meaning in all of life's relationships. To write one's spiritual biography without prayer is beyond imagination. To turn life from frustrations and futilities of external preoccupations to the center of meaning and life is the compelling need of our day. Only then can people find the creative self, the spiritual being, the personal history worthy of the rewriting.

34. CREATING A RESONANT BEING

As with any great art, prayer always demands more of us than a discipline. From the discipline we achieve must come the fine fruits of a divine resonance. That is, we so completely lose ourselves in the presence of the Divine Nature that we become quickly and readily responsive to the divine will. We achieve a sense of unity between the man and his maker, the creature and his Creator, the cosmically established design and our expression of it. In this kind of prayer great listening takes place, but it is not listening that craves an echo of itself, but rather employment of the self that has been made resonant by preparation and desire.

One of the dangers of the listening posture in prayer comes when there appears to be nothing but a void. We assume the role of the listener and then adjust ourselves to an emptiness that seems to encompass creation. During such moments it is most hazardous to judge the silences, for we may say with good intent, and sad deception, "There is no God." In one way this violates the Commandment about taking the name of God in vain. To pray out of our emptiness, to open ourselves as if to hear and then have no capacity to hear, is spiritual frustration in the extreme.

The disciplined spirit that prepares itself to wait upon the Lord does not engage in the use of inverted prayer power. When a child is born, the effort is strenuous. The being that has been engaged in the cosmic partnership that creates new life fulfills the demands placed upon it by a final, painful, but fruitful effort. A new soul is born. The spiritual growth process calls for a creative yet painful act to harbor the divine in the effort to make the human responsive not to the self, but to the Beyond-Self. Growth makes demands on life. To become aware and responsive to the demands of the spirit is a process like unto birth. This need for rebirth at the spiritual level was recognized by our Master. We cannot live well without it. We can recognize why the resonance created by prayer may be the instrument to assist in this rebirth of being.

The practical aspects of the matter can be easily demonstrated. We have watched personalities injured by life retreat into the negative satisfactions of self-pity. When the pity-centered self dominates life, it becomes increasingly difficult to see anything that does not degenerate into intensified self-pity. Finally such a life finds no satisfaction except in its own self-degradation, and its whining attitude makes it more difficult to generate the health of spirit and group relations that could result in more abundant living. So self-pity moves one from poverty of spirit to greater isolation of spirit, until the possibilities for achieving resonance to something vital beyond the self are atrophied.

Just so does the complacent self immerse itself in the satisfactions that begin and end with the individual and his small world. Increasingly the experiences that could enrich life are excluded by the unseeing attitude he allows to dominate his thought. He becomes a man of his own thoughts, little, narrow, cramped, intolerant, seeking little from others and able to share even less with them. The mood of withdrawal into small ideas about life leads to the place where the resonance of being no longer exists, and that man is reduced to dwarflike proportions in feeling and life experience.

In similar fashion the arrogant self exerts its strong will on all others. Increasingly, his will is dominant, and little place is accorded to man or God unless they can be fitted into the scheme of his arrogance. So he rules out of life all that would help his spirit grow, and hurries impoverished toward his unlamented grave.

The self that is ridden with guilt and condemnation is increasingly cut off from the healthy interrelation with others because it keeps projecting its feelings into the feelings and thoughts of others and gets little back except that which increases the feeling of guilt. Again, the ideas that dominate life very quickly become the major portion of life.

But life need not be dominated by these deadly and crippling selves. The dedicated life moves beyond self-interest in its concern for others. The complacent self may become stirred with vision of needs so great that he can never be satisfied again with things as they are. The arrogant self may come face to face with something so beautiful and wonderful that he falls in humility and from that time on seeks a will beyond his own. And the guilt-ridden soul may find forgiveness so that he can look at his own life with a feeling of freedom and cleanness within, and in so doing can look at others with joy and value their worthiness.

Our worries and our fears do not fulfill life, for they chain it to unworthy preoccupations. But the very elements of traditional prayer place before us the resources that break the narrow molds within which the small ideas of men would bring suffocation.

What happens to self-pity when a person prays with the real joy of thanksgiving? Perspective is changed, blessings appear where least expected, and life becomes a thing of joy and wonder.

What happens when the self-willed person bows in confession? He sees himself as he is. He measures himself by a will beyond his own. He sees the weakness of his ways and returns to the disciplined life that is subject to a higher will.

What happens when the complacent person looks to God in prayer? He cannot help but look within himself. He cannot help but see values beyond the poverty of ideas that has cramped his life. The hard shell of his selfish satisfaction is broken open by his new understanding. He begins to live anew.

What happens when the person steeped in self-condemnation finds the satisfaction of God's redeeming and forgiving love made real to him? He no longer finds satisfaction in guilt feelings or self-condemnation, but rises above it in joy and appreciation of the restoration of his self-regard.

So also those who have been drowning in their self-consciousness can lift their petitions for release from this plague of seeing themselves wherever they look. How monotonous it must be to live a life surrounded by mirrors and with no windows. God-consciousness opens windows to life and makes it possible for the self to become an instrument on the way to something worthy rather than a dead end of a hopeless journey.

If the law of the mind and spirit are so clearly at work in our lives, why should there be any hesitancy or delay in applying them? Why do we not immediately apply them and discover the satisfactions that result?

The discouraging truth is that these laws are demanding. Man did not overcome the law of gravity until he had developed the type of machine and equipment that could fly. But then he was only learning to cooperate with the laws that had previously thwarted his efforts. The laws of the spirit also make their demands, and our minds must meet the requirements before they can be fulfilled.

Our age is marked by a fear of the contemplative life. Giant strides have been taken in the world of externals, but we have just begun to be aware of how slowly we have moved in things of the spirit. We fear being alone. In an experiment with a group of students, an effort was made to evaluate their response to solitude. They were provided with adequate food and everything needed for bodily comfort. But they were denied radios, television sets, and all forms of escapist literature. Instead, they were provided with literary classics. At the end of three days spent in solitary confinement 90 per cent of the students were in a state of acute panic, and the other 10 per cent reported that they had had a trying experience. Those who can be alone with themselves and be at ease and enjoy themselves represent a very small minority. How can those who fear solitude even under pleasant circumstances look with ease on the discipline of contemplation and creative silence which is so much a part of prayer?

More than we dare think, ours is a day of automatic actions. We are conditioned by the many forces that play upon our minds. What we say and do is precalculated by such powerful forces of modern life that there seems to be little place for the reaction of the self that is free to respond to its own deeper sensitivities. The fear of spontaneity threatens the fulfillment of the self. So we live a life cramped and marred by so many defects that it takes a highly cultivated set of defenses to make the life tolerable. But we cannot ignore the stirrings of the soul that is made in God's image.

In the face of these conditions, it will take more than a logical acceptance of the power of prayer to fulfill and transform life. It will take a Herculean effort to break the chains that bind our minds. This can come only with a desire and an effort compatible with the desire.

So we can set the goals for the development of the life of our spirits and then employ the methods that can lead to that end.

Such goals will lead against the major emphases of life in our day. A new value on individualism will have to emerge.

The oppression of thought and feeling, the hierarchy of economic and social values, the submission of mind and heart to commercialized necessity will have to give way to an all-encompassing attention to the Divine Nature. Inner discipline, conscience, reason, and the belief in the sanctity of the individual will have to assert themselves again.

The soul at prayer is the soul standing at attention before God. It is prepared to amplify the still, small voice until it sounds like a mighty roar. Simone Weil wrote of the efforts to bring the whole being to attention so that it may put its complete resources of concentration, contemplation, and concern at the disposal of God. The resonant being is the one prepared to listen to the God who is prepared to communicate his will.

35. THE POWER TO BECOME

❧

WE live in a power-conscious age. We have more horsepower at our disposal for the ordinary tasks of life than any previous era in history. We have so much nuclear power in reserve stockpiles that it poses more of a threat than a consolation. Considerable loose thinking about the nature of this power and the moral obligations concerning its use deserve the immediate and prayerful attention of all mankind.

Because man uses so much power now, we falsely assume that man creates power. No man ever creates even a fraction of a horsepower of real energy. He uses it, he transforms it, he modifies it, but he does not create it. All power is of God. It is the raw material of creation itself.

It makes little difference whether the energy comes from coal buried deep in the earth millions of years ago, or from petroleum stored in great underground reservoirs untold ages ago, or the energy created by water rushing over the waterfall—none of it is manmade. The energy in the coal was gathered millennia ago by living matter which took it from the sun. The oil in the earth was also living matter which used the same cosmic sources of energy when it was alive. Even the water that creates power as it falls in the river has been drawn from the sea by the sun and is carried over the land by cloud and wind to be released over mountains, rivers, and plains in form of snow or rain. Here is energy to be sure, power for the use of man, but none of it was made by man.

What shall we say of a man's physical power, his own brute strength? Whence this power that enables him to lift heavy weights, to jump hurdles, and run the mile in record time? Where does your energy come from? The answer is that you have the gift of life and it is sustained by a continuous source of interstellar energy. You eat the vegetables and fruits that grow in the earth. Their energy comes from the sun, the rain, and the chemicals of the earth. Or, if you neglect vegetables and fruit, you eat beef, lamb, or fowl, in which instance you are receiving the energy resources that cows, sheep, and chickens have stored for you. No matter how you examine it, you find that man with his wisdom and skills transforms energy and uses it for his purposes, but he never creates it. Power is.

We may misuse power. We may waste the energy of life. We may threaten civilization by our unwise use of nuclear energy. Many of us have more power than intelligence. A woman may fret and worry herself into a headache by unwise living. Then she may take a two-ton car with 300 horsepower and use it to drive a half mile to the store to buy an ounce of medication to relieve the headache she didn't have to have if she had learned to live more wisely. So much of life is characterized by the unwise use of both our inner and outer resources.

This certainly is true of the spiritual energy that is the power of prayer. In the prologue of John's Gospel there is a statement to those who believe Jesus will give the power to become the sons of God. This appears to mean that those who learn how to use spiritual power will be made close relatives of the source of this energy. They will in effect share the wonders and mysteries of creation.

Jesus speaks of spiritual power as if it were similar in nature but different in kind from other types of energy. It is similar in nature because spiritual power too is an endowment. It is not created by man. It is similar in nature because we are endowed with ability to use it, though we do not make it. It is different in kind because it is an inner resource and not external. It is different in kind because it calls for an inner discipline to use it rather than external devices to transform it.

The coal and oil in the earth lay there for untold centuries as a source of power, but the power was potential and did not become actual until man developed skills that could transform it from its crude form to the refined states which were necessary for its use. Nuclear energy has been sustaining life on the face of the earth since its beginning, for the sun runs its heating and lighting facilities from this power source. But we knew little about it and, even though our lives depended upon it, we did not even begin to understand it. Only within recent decades have we gained some knowledge of this endless source of energy. It took the bringing together of the refined skills of many great intellects in mathematics, physics, and applied engineering to release this newly discovered source of power. Now we can use it or abuse it. Which it is will depend upon yet another form of power we must learn to use.

Prayer can be the instrument by which the spiritual power which is potential in every individual is made actual. The power is, but it is necessary for it to "become" in the individual.

John Wesley placed emphasis on the ideal of perfection. It is the process of becoming. He spoke of going on to perfection as if it were a never-ending process. One never fulfills the full possibilities of his being, but he is continually engaged in the process of achieving his own perfectibility. The use of prayer is the point in life where the individual focuses his attention on his spiritual potential so that the power that is in him is transformed from its native state, its potentiality, into its realized state, its actuality. This is a strenuous process demanding all there is in a person. Just as physical power is transformed through engineering skills and technical ability, so the spiritual power may be transformed from an unrealized endowment to a fact of life.

John Wesley felt that this process must be carried on at several levels of being simultaneously. At the intellectual level it was made possible through the discovery of truth. This truth of which he spoke was more than merely the acquiring of facts, for it demanded the wisdom that puts facts together in a pattern of wise meanings. Only when this was done was the mind able to engage itself in the process of perfectibility.

At the physical level this demanded discipline of time, muscular energy, and unending dedication to worthy goals. It is not easy to get up at four o'clock in the morning, as Wesley did, to meditate, study the Scriptures, and pray, but without the necessary discipline of energy and time the other benefits could not be made available. Living as we do in a different era, we have a different time schedule. When there was little artificial light people went to bed early and could arise at an early hour. We may have to adapt the time schedule to our special needs today, but there is no substitute for the determined effort to make such time available. John Wesley extended this discipline almost compulsively to other aspects of his behavior. He drove himself through fifty years of active ministry wisely to discipline his time and energy as one of the important parts of his perfectibility.

But in addition to the mental and physical ordering of his life, he added the achieving of piety as the fulfillment of his spiritual nature. For him piety was not an expression of a sanctimonious attitude of life. He was a practical man and went to people with his message wherever he found them, but he felt that a spiritual sensitivity to God's will was essential to bring the other qualities of perfectibility to their highest point of realization.

To this end, Wesley tried to recognize the spiritual worth of all men, whatever their station in life. He was sensitive to the potential in all men seeking to become actual. When thugs tried to break up his meetings for amusement, he went directly to the leader of the gang, looked him straight in the eye, and told him he was concerned for the welfare of his soul. This could be quite disarming to those who had never realized that they had a soul worthy of concern. Often those who came to disrupt his meetings went away convinced in their own hearts that they had a divine nature, and that it could be used for creative goals rather than for destructive amusement. This concern for the unrealized spiritual power in those he ministered to became an important factor in changing the spiritual climate of England.

The power to become found its finest realization in the achieving of divine sonship. Traditionally this was spoken of as the indwelling of the Holy Spirit. Actually in more modern terms it could be spoken of as the transforming of the potential power of the individual into a life-changing use of that power to modify attitudes and behavior because of a new awareness of relationship between the creature and the Creator. So it was that John Wesley employed prayer as a powerful instrument toward the goal of achieved meaning in life. For him prayer was not so much an end in itself as it was a means to that end. Just as he saw the church as an instrument to change men, so also he used prayer as the means for change. In the quiet processes of self-examination, men looked within and found an undiscovered reservoir of power, waiting to be mined, pumped out, or refined so that its influences could be used to remake the goals and attitudes of life. In this sense prayer became the transformer of spiritual power.

In our power-conscious age, we have too long failed to realize the importance of this undeveloped spiritual energy. Our preoccupation with external power has tended to make us an outer-motivated people. But our use of outer power can bring disaster if we cannot learn how to employ the inner-motivating powers that can exert significant controls on the external world we have developed. When Jesus worked with men he did it with a consciousness of reserves of faith, love, and goodness that most people ignored.

One of the important fruits of prayer can be the new awareness of the inner kingdom with its power. When we learn to transform this from potential to actual, we will have taken a long step toward actualizing the power to become the sons of God.

36. THE KEY TO WHOLENESS

ONE of the tragedies of our age is that we have become so specialized in so many ways that disintegration has set in in the lives of individuals, religious groups, and social organizations. We have organized ourselves about the fragments of life and so have failed to find significant organization, and in its place have produced fragmentation.

In an era when there is great advancement in medical science, there is more evidence of breakdown in physical and emotional functioning than ever before. We know more and more about isolated details of living, but less and less about the important meanings and relationships that can hold life together.

We do not like to be compared with rats, but those who make clinical studies of animal behavior say that there are many comparable traits shared by men and rats. In our casual speech we sometimes admit that there are some men who act like rats. A group of scientists studying the will to live did experiments with rats to determine what gave them a determination to struggle for life, and what appeared to be the cause of their disintegration of purpose for living. In one of the experiments they placed some sound, healthy, well-integrated rats in vats of water to see how long they could swim or float before they gave up the struggle for life and drowned. The rats swam from sixty to eighty hours before giving up.

A similar group of rats, just as healthy, well-fed, and integrated, were placed in similar vats, with one significant difference; they had their whiskers cut off. The rats' whiskers are their chief contact with the world about them. They provide sensory clues to the spatial and object relationship between the rats and their world. The behavior of these rats was quite different. Some of them were dead within ten minutes and none of them showed half the will to live, the will to struggle for life that the first group had shown. For them, in truth, life was hanging by a whisker.

Without trying to overgeneralize or attach too much significance to a whisker, I think we can see that when relationship is destroyed, when the contact with familiar and meaningful things is broken, the will to live is affected, life becomes disorganized, and energy is disintegrated.

Power that is not used violates itself. The power for meaningful life, when dissipated in meaningless activity, debilitates life. The loss of meaning for life and the nihilism so characteristic of our age combine to speed the process of disintegration of life that leads to tragic personal and social results.

If a businessman has no greater purpose in life than the accumulation of wealth, his life bogs down in the loss of significant relationships; like the whiskerless rats, he tends to abandon his values and goals, and sinks into the morass of small thinking and small acting.

A writer who has trained strenuously to produce copy of the highest literary worth may become responsible for the preparation of a daily syndicated column. Under the pressures of such a schedule he may lose his capacity for artful expression, and in time sink into the patterns of verbose and meaningless verbalizations. He may well have lost something that he can never restore.

Without realizing it, many persons have become ensnared in the worship of money and things. They are in danger of destroying themselves by the worship of graven images. Material power, human reason, and organizational strength also become images beguiling the mind.

What happens to the individual can also happen to the church when it becomes more interested in size, materialistic measurements, and social prestige than in truth, human values, and divine imperatives. The institution that preaches the dignity of man, and brotherhood, and then practices the type of discrimination that puts superficial things first is well on the way to losing its soul. The class-conscious church with a country-club atmosphere can hardly claim to be representative of the living body of Christ.

The institutions of special interests that seek social change based on resentment, conflict, and hatred of man for man produce evil fruits. Jesus spoke of the prayerful discipline that loves enemies, and does good for those who abuse. Only actions based on small purposes disintegrate, whereas the goals set by high purposes may produce suffering or even death itself; they nonetheless integrate life toward the purposes that are of supreme worth. Jesus knew that abuses could long be expected, but his teaching in the Beatitudes makes it clear that he sees no alternative for his followers but to accept and work toward these higher purposes regardless of the consequences.

The Quakers have demonstrated the social power of the prayerful approach to life. Any church that in times of crisis and decision neglects the true source of its spiritual values has already sold its birthright for a mess of pottage. But the church that looks to the courageous example of Christ and gives up the superficial elements of its program and life to preserve values for which Christ died will truly share in his life and rise up in newness of life as a congregation.

One of the manifestations of spiritual power is found in the achievement of true wholeness—personally, socially, and spiritually. What then is the key to wholeness in a world where disintegration displaces integration, and material values inundate the values of the spirit?

Jesus repeatedly pointed out that the individual was made whole through his faith. When his faith in himself and in the spiritual power God had invested in him failed, life lost its meaning and he lost his will to live significantly. He then reverted to the subsistence level of the animal or the vegetable. When his faith was restored he responded to the power of his Creator, and became a new creature. This new power within manifested itself in his health, his behavior, and his basic attitudes. He became a new man in Christ Jesus.

Life of the first-century church revealed this power in dramatic form. Discouraged and bereft of faith, the followers of Jesus wandered aimlessly after his death. They did not know whether to return to their homes and former pursuits or to remain in Jerusalem. At Pentecost their faith was born anew through the indwelling of the Holy Spirit. From that moment on the disintegrated fellowship became a living institution with a complete renewal of faith and purpose. Although internal and external problems plagued the followers from time to time, they now had a goal large enough to integrate their community of faith, and give it wholeness. That initial impulse, dramatized in field and dungeon, shipwreck and persecution, was a life-giving force that motivates the church even in our day. The key to the life of the early church was its dedication to purpose, its discipline in prayer and devotion.

Some who explore the deep recesses of the souls of men feel that deep within is a place of horror and savagery. Those who believe that man is made in the image of God feel that in the depth of his being is a treasure house of spiritual energy waiting to be unlocked and opened. But where is the key? Can access be gained by way of the powerful forces created by men's engineering and scientific skill? Can the lock be picked by the clever escape artists who would find the riches without accepting the responsibilities?

No, the course into the treasure house of being is not found by force or subterfuge. Rather, the key is made available to all who would learn the discipline of spirit that would open the doors. Prayer is the instrument that awakens man to the values within. Prayer brings attention to a focus that reveals the whole person, the whole church, and the whole society.

When George Washington Carver sought scientific ways to redeem the economy of the South, he employed his skills as a botanist and his spiritual sensitivity to accomplish his goals. In prayerful contemplation God urged him to devote full attention to a peanut and hear what it had to say. He listened attentively, and discovered the key principle that unlocked a whole new world of usefulness hitherto concealed in this lowly vegetable. His discoveries resulted in 240 new products, and did much to bring diversified production in a one-crop economy that had plagued the South.

In the processes of prayerful attention can be found the keys to personal and social problems, individual and collective crises. The power of God is continually at work to reveal his wonders and mysteries to those who will pay attention. Wholeness is not a mystery to be achieved through tranquilizers or externally applied medication. Rather, it is a product of meaningful faith. When we find that meaning, we have the key to our wholeness as persons, a living church, and a creative society.

37. PRAYER AND GUIDANCE

❧❦❧

GUIDANCE has gained stature among people who admit to confusion and seek to resolve their inner conflicts. The use of vocational guidance tests helps to determine one's capabilities for various types of employment. Placement tests give clues to the varied talents that may not have been ascertained in ordinary experience. In effect, persons look outside themselves for an understanding of their inner resources. Personality tests and measurements have come into their own to provide source material for people considering a choice of life vocation, job placement, or job relocation.

Similarly, when people are confronted with personality problems, they have increasingly turned to professional counselors for direction and help. In this process, the counselee seeks aid in respect to the image of the self, the source and nature of the problem, and the approach most likely to succeed in resolving the problem.

A whole new profession has grown up in mass media through which perplexed persons write to a columnist, state their problem, and then receive a cryptic reply intended to ease the burden quickly and painlessly. Many persons only add to their state of confusion by reading a variety of these comments that seldom go to the heart of the problem that is intensely and peculiarly personal.

However, many persons confused and uncertain about life's

problems look outward for answers that ultimately can only be found within. A psychiatrist who had spent twenty-five years helping people said that he never had as a patient anyone who had really learned the art and discipline of prayer. In effect, he was saying that people under the discipline of prayer are whole and have no need of the physician.

As one who has been engaged in pastoral counseling for many years and has spent many thousands of hours in face-to-face encounter with troubled and confused persons, I am not inclined to downgrade the benefits that can come through wise and competent psychotherapy. But I am inclined to think that the benefits of counseling might not be necessary if there were a more adequate prayer life practiced by persons who were trying to find their way in life.

Immediately there will be those who say that they have always prayed and still have had the problems that lead to mental and emotional breakdown. This may well be true, but it is my feeling that two reasons exist for this apparent failure. One is that what is often considered to be prayer falls short of the ideal of effective prayer already discussed. The second reason is that the clear insight that may have come through prayer has been ignored because it was too demanding. Too often people seek quick and easy answers through prayer as an external manipulation of life, rather than a dedicating of self to a demanding inner discipline that could transform the life of a person willing to pay the price.

Many of those saintly souls who have represented the highest form of prayer have learned their inner discipline from a master at prayer who called himself a spiritual guide. He did not specialize in psychological testing, or external standards of measurement. Rather, he steadfastly explored deeper and deeper into the spiritual resources of his nature in the quest for that inner kingdom that brought him to know the genius of his own nature as a spiritual being.

Martin Luther, John Knox, Baron von Hügel, and Evelyn Underhill carried on lengthy and illuminating correspondence with those whom they served as spiritual guides. Through these many pages of creative correspondence they constantly emphasized the importance of turning inward, not to find the surface self that they already knew, but that deeper and more profound spiritual self that had to be wooed into life.

This spiritual self is the evidence of man's nature as a supernatural being. All ultimate truth comes from the supernatural sources. All ultimate truth starts with the subjective and moves toward its objectivization. The subjective is the deep within. It is the fulfillment of the possibility for God-consciousness.

We tend to be so preoccupied with the objective that we accept it as the only reality. This applies even to our confused concepts of the church as a living body or a fellowship of believers. The same margin for error occurs in thinking of our bodies as temples rather than meeting places for encounter and renewal.

If we are to achieve the benefits of spiritual guidance we must start at the point of spiritual acceptance. The objectivization of so much of life works against this possibility. We get lost in the dualism of inner and outer, real and unreal. We completely overlook the fundamental principle that life is unity at the deepest level of spiritual meaning. The acceptance of ourselves as spiritual beings is the point at which we can begin to give the ultimate of meaning to all the rest of living. This calls for a special kind of humility.

Simone Weil defines it in this way, "Humanity is the refusal to exist outside God."[1] God as the ultimate of spiritual meaning pervades all there is—body, mind, and spirit—and gives to all of life a unity achieved through its spiritual purpose. T. S.

[1] Marie M. Davy, *The Mysticism of Simone Weil* (Boston: Beacon Press, 1951), p. 30.

Eliot puts it in this way, "The only wisdom we can hope to acquire is the wisdom of humility; humility is endless."[2] These are but the varied ways of saying that spiritual meaning for existence is found at the point where we admit to ourselves that all there is is one in God. Once we accept this fact with all its meaning, we realize that all of our experience is bound together in an ultimate meaning that is an endless revelation of God's purpose which becomes evident to those under the discipline of humility. This is the ultimate of self-acceptance.

When we make this act of self-acceptance we cease the frenzied effort to bend life to its lesser meanings. We seek only the ultimate meaning, and, as one spiritual genius put it, "We drive with slack reins." When we are not sure of the way, we can give the horse his head, relax the tension on the reins, and the horse will use his sixth sense to find the way. Guidance that comes through spiritual sensitivity is expressed at the point in life where we let up on the reins of self-direction and quietly wait for that source of direction within ourselves to assert itself.

A scientific researcher seeking to understand the phenomena of spiritual guidance made a careful study of a number of persons who had practiced the discipline. He found that his subjects had developed a sixth sense that was available in times of need. At first the sixth sense was not sure of itself and was at times confusing and uncertain. But as the humility of life was practiced, and the extensions of the self and its limited interests were controlled, this inner sensitivity grew and asserted itself with increasing authority.

In a time when we are increasingly aware of the needs for guidance, and in general practice look to others for practical insight, it may be important to explore again the responsiveness to the inner and subjective sense of what is true for aid.

[2] *East Coker*, quoted in Davy, *loc. cit.*

The lie detector works on the premise that everyone has a built-in truth meter. When the truth is violated the body involuntarily reacts in a manner that can be measured. The senses through the skin, the vascular system through blood pressure, and the autonomic nervous system through the heart record the responsiveness of the total organism to truth and falsehood.

Inner spiritual truth appears to have a similar type of built-in response. As God is truth, the being that learns to open itself quietly to that truth receives its input.

The arts of true prayer are the best means by which the individual develops his sensitivity. Such prayer is the device by which he makes his whole being responsive to the inner kingdom that would assert itself and give direction to life, if and when it is given the opportunity. In our outer-motivated mode of life, it is doubly important for us to cultivate this inner sensitivity so that it is able to bring its spiritual guidance again into life.

However, lest we think this is something that can happen quickly and easily, we need to be warned that it is the end result of a long and demanding quest that brings to life deep within us a spiritual nature that too often lies dormant. Perhaps one of the great difficulties of finding God is that God is carried within the self. Perhaps one of the reasons that we fail to find the guidance of God is that we look outward rather than within.

The discipline of prayer may well be the best way open to us to discover the guidance God would give. Then the finest fruits of the spirit's life can be realized in the unity of being that brings the God-self into fulfillment through the full acceptance of ourselves as spiritual beings made in the image of God, and seeking in humility to bring that image to fulfillment in the total fabric of our lives.

38. PRAYER: A CHANNEL OF REVELATION

❦

WE have already made the point that revelation is a way God's truth is made known to man directly. In this chapter we want to extend the boundaries of this definition. We have made clear our belief that prayer is the depth dimension of the spirit's life. This is far more than a matter of sound psychological principle. At the same time, there is no violation of psychological insights. What we propose is beyond investigation techniques available to laboratory science. It is in effect the fulfillment of all that science, philosophy, or religion could reveal if raised to a higher power.

Prayer does not violate reason, but it is not limited by reason. Reason is a function of the mind, but prayer uses the totality of being. Revelation is more than sensory response to stimuli. It involves mental and spiritual powers unlimited by sensory perception.

A physical dimension exists in prayer, but it is certainly not all there is of prayer. When I pray with a patient in the hospital, I usually take one of the patient's hands in mine and place my other hand on the patient's forehead. This warmth and directness of human contact communicates nonverbally, and produces responses that are difficult to explain on the basis of sensory response alone. Something deeper appears to be communicated from the spirit of one praying human to the spirit of another. The body contact enhances a relationship that already exists and uses it to reveal powers and meanings that only then and under those immediate conditions are revealed.

The physical dimension of revealed meaning is added to by capacities of the mind's life that are beyond easy comprehension. Religion has always made room for the vision, the divinely inspired imagination, the psychic phenomenon. In recent years this confident acceptance on the part of religion has been justified and confirmed by scientific studies on the nature of consciousness. The small portion of the mind's life that is within the bounds of consciousness is immersed in other mental activities that are referred to as the unconscious, preconscious, and superconscious. Too often our preoccupation with the lower levels of consciousness has limited or denied our sensitivity to that equally valid and religiously more important portion of the mind's life that appears to be concerned with revelation. The ability of some portion of the mind to function beyond the limits of space and time, to be aware of dimensions of existence that are not limited by manmade measurements of convenience, is increasingly a source of study. These newly revealed insights make it obvious that what has long been observed as a religious phenomenon can be in part explained by our understanding of the mental equipment of man.

Telepathic studies carried on under laboratory controlled conditions show that it is possible for the human mind to be aware of information, facts, and experience that are revealed not through the physical senses, but rather through a totality of being functioning above and beyond the so-called normal. This paranormal function has been shown to be related to a variety of factors.

Studies of spontaneous clairvoyant and clairaudient experiences show that they usually take place where there are strong emotional ties at work. They occur most frequently among husbands and wives, parents and children, brothers and sisters. These experiences rarely occur among casual acquaintances or people with little concern one for the other.

Other studies show that there is a clear relationship between these unusual capacities and the basic mental capacities of the people directly involved. People with high intelligence are more likely to experience them than those of lesser endowment.

It has also been established that there is a personality quotient at work to explain the capacity. Persons with an open, optimistic, affirmative view of life are more inclined to experience these phenomena than persons who are suspicious, doubt-filled, and resistant to human communication.

One study that set out to disprove any telepathic capability of man ended an eleven-year study by frankly denying its original premise. This study asserted the interesting fact that belief was a measurable factor in telepathic responsiveness. Those who believed in the possibility of telepathic communication scored above chance in the testing about the same percentage as those who disbelieved in it scored below chance. Not only was it discovered that belief was a measurable factor in mental activity, but also that disbelief was equally significant in relation to the end result of the studies.

Studies of children as they entered public school were compared with studies of the same children taken after they had been in school for two years. It was found that at the beginning they had a considerably higher capacity for extrasensory perception than they had at the end of two years of schooling. Evidently the socializing process and the increased dependence upon verbal communication and social approval led to a withering away of a natural endowment.

A similar study of school children in seven states and including many thousands of children showed that where the children felt a warm and friendly relationship with the teacher the learning process was stimulated. Where there was a feeling of distrust, antagonism, and mutual rejection between teacher and pupil there was a measurable resistance to learning and a retarding of the kind of communication that led to fruitful acquiring of specific knowledge.

What does all of this mean? It appears to mean that there is a correlation of emotional factors and the subtle processes of the mind that affect what we call sensitivity to revealed truth. It further appears to be true that mental and personality attributes have a bearing upon the total functioning of a person in relation to this specialized sensitivity. Belief, desire, and feelings of love are as significant in terms of the end result as disbelief, disinterest, and emotional states of personal rejection and insecurity.

The implication is that special sensitivity may be developed or destroyed, in part at least, by variables in the emotional and spiritual environment of the individual. The capacity to believe greatly releases mental energies in the life of a person that can stimulate his so-called spiritual sensitivity. The proper climate of worship, meditation, and mental conditioning that makes one feel secure and significantly related to cosmic sources of truth may well produce the fine fruits of that relationship through experiences of revelation.

Students endowed with that mysterious quality we call genius affirm that "the genius" appears to have a built-in sensitivity that enables them to know almost instantaneously what other people have to work hard to achieve. Some who are spiritually sensitive appear to have a capacity to enter into meaningful relationship with a cosmic consciousness that can reveal insight, understanding, and wisdom about the essential truth of creation. This cosmic consciousness appears to be the active agent in the experiences of the mystics and the saints who through strenuous effort and audacious faith have used their human resources to open the way for insight into the ultimate truth of creation. When this phenomenon occurs we speak of it as revelation. It does not deny any truth revealed to the senses, but adds to it a quality of meaning which is beyond the capacity of the senses to acquire.

True revelation is the fulfillment of reason, the achievement of life's thirsting after the more abundant life. It is the point at which creature-consciousness merges with the cosmic consciousness to share the understandings that are the evidence of prayer's finest realization.

Quite obviously this revelation is the source of ultimate truth. It cannot be discovered in the world of external things, for it is not of that world. It is found through the resources of the inner kingdom that are cultivated resources. There is no final spiritual guidance apart from this truth that is achieved through revelation. When it is discovered it becomes the greatest good.

It moves beyond the distinctions of measurement and the distinctions that are the preoccupation of the merely rational processes. The highest form of the religious consciousness comes with the great both-ands of life where the artificial judgments between animate and inanimate, object and subject, time and eternity, space and the infinite, creature and Creator are fulfilled in an awareness that can no longer be satisfied with the trivial either-ors of life that tend to divide and disintegrate the understanding of it.

The finest fruits of prayer come to life when the disciplining of the spirit produces those conditions where the person is able to believe audaciously, feel loved and secure in the midst of cosmic forces, feel open and responsive to the truth that can come flooding in upon him when he determines not to resist it, but rather to make himself accessible to it. This prayer as the finest achievement of the integrated and integrating individual combines the best of psychological and psychical endowment, and uses it as the launching pad to set the spirit in the orbit of cosmic truth. This prayer is the point at which the questing spirit of man and the revealing spirit of God become one in the highest achievement of the religious consciousness.

39. WHAT JESUS TAUGHT ABOUT PRAYER

WE recognize Jesus as the great Master of Prayer. Most of the insights that we have presented in the pages that preceded this chapter have been built upon the insights he has bequeathed us. Now we would try to summarize his thought and action concerning prayer more concretely.

What Jesus taught about prayer is revealed not so much through what he said as in what he was. For him prayer was a way of life. The insight he gave his disciples in the recipe for prayer has often been used as a formal prayer itself without regard to his warning against vain repetition. If we would seek the meaning of the recipe, we would probably best find it by moving beyond the words themselves to the meanings that underlie them.

His way of life shown in his prayerful attitude toward the gift of life he treasured in himself and others starts with the recognition that cosmic power can be made personal. The stance of prayer is that of the worshipful mood. It is expressed through a quest for the inner kingdom where divine sovereignty may be fulfilled for each individual. The ultimate meaning of that sovereignty comes when the divine will becomes one with the human energy that accepts it and fulfills it. This is done both in doing and being. Nothing is excluded, for it starts with the material things that sustain life itself. It moves quickly to a recognition of a reciprocal relationship that shares the grace of God in giving to others the future that we seek for ourselves, for without that reciprocity of spirit there is no true awareness of God's grace for us. This grace becomes real for each person at the point where he is willing to accept the full meaning of divine guidance and the great affirmation of faith that through that guidance we find deliverance from all that would plague the life of the spirit. This willingness to be guided into salvation and deliverance opens the doors to the inner kingdom that is truly God's, and within which is revealed the power and the glory that is man's great spiritual achievement. When this is found it brings to life a focus upon the infinite that is not measured by time, but which brings the eternal into life now. Through this mode of prayer may be found the way of life he sought for his followers, for he took it as his mission to reveal within time the life that was eternal.

This emphasis on the inner kingdom and its power brought Jesus into conflict with a tradition that had been deeply rooted in the forms and rituals employed in worship and generally accepted as prayer. This thin veneer of whitewash over the corrupted natures of men fell far short of his ideal, and he warned against the hazard of confusing the superficial ways of worship with the inner quality of life that showed what was really going on in the life of a man.

When he spoke of the inner kingdom, he was misunderstood. Those who heard him proclaim an intimate relationship to the God within considered him blasphemous. Ultimately they put him to death for what they considered to be his unwarranted presumption. They did not realize that his desire to make all of life subject to God's will was the ultimate of humility rather than an expression of arrogance. He makes this clear in his teaching.

In the familiar Beatitudes, Jesus delineates the way toward a responsive self. Starting with humility, which is the prime requisite of teachability, he equates an awareness of spiritual need with the awakening of that inner spiritual kingdom which is the earthly counterpart of the realm where the cosmic spiritual nature exists. Such willingness to learn opens wide the doors. Such humility before spiritual truth makes it possible for one to approach the spiritual kingdom deep within which is man's special endowment.

Then Jesus moves immediately to the subject of creative suffering in its most acute form, the adjustment to deprivation caused by death. This forces man to contemplate both the full meaning of his mortal nature and divine possibility. When one is engaged in the work of mourning, he is dealing with the essential relationships that bind life to life, though he is obliged to contemplate not so much the physical as the spiritual. In this contemplation he finds a new sense of relationship that brings perspective and comfort, the manifestations of spiritual strength in the midst of mortal suffering.

When Jesus speaks of meekness he does not mean weakness. He is thinking rather of the controlled strength that is capable of submitting itself to something larger than itself. This suppressed strength as an inherited discipline increases the boundaries of the promised land to encompass the whole earth.

Spiritual sensitivity without moral concern may be dangerous. True spiritual satisfaction comes to those whose beings cry out in their basic desire for God, their hungering and thirsting for his being within their being. The self responds, not only to its need, but also to a clearly defined framework of values that undergirds the fulfillment and the satisfaction of those needs.

The responsive self is always able to relate its needs and desires to the needs and desires of others. Its judgments grow from compassion. Its feelings for others are rooted in empathic responses. It is able to "sit where they sit." Not in pity, but in mercy, it fosters a creative relationship that nourishes the bonds between soul and soul, and heals as it is healed, sustains as it is sustained, and exalts as it is exalted.

"Out of the heart come the issues of life." The motivation of life is of prime importance for its expression. Love cannot grow from hate, nor confidence from suspicion. God's nature as infinite love is revealed to those who approach life with uncomplicated motives, with purity of purpose. The responsive self is a loving self.

Peace is the atmosphere of the responsive self. The reconciling, understanding concern for others creates the mood of patience rather than petulance, reconciliation rather than retaliation, and consideration rather than condemnation. This mood makes men brothers through their common submission to an authority found in a common spiritual sonship.

Nor does Jesus ignore the fact that such a spiritual view of life in a world of people motivated by other concerns is dangerous and perhaps fatal at the physical level. Jewish history had made that clear before. But the glory of spiritual achievement cannot be diverted by the consequences that may well come from it, for the rewards are not material but spiritual.

Jesus was quite practical about the ways people could work out their struggle for humility. If they sought rewards they found them at the level of their seeking. If they sought honor among men, they would find it there. But if their quest was for the sovereignty of God in all of life, no other source of satisfaction was important to them. So if in preparation for prayer they remembered fractured human relationships with relative, neighbor, or friend, this became the first claim upon their attention, for they must seek reconciliation before they approached the altar.

We do not begin to understand the incidents in the life of Jesus or the impact of his life upon mankind ever since unless we see that all that he was and did was the determined effort to work out the implications of the life of prayer in the affairs of men. He did not seek exemption from human stress or suffering. He claimed again and again that he was the Son of man, for he did not want to separate his living witness from the context of human experience. In fact, he claimed repeatedly that what he did others could do if they would submit themselves to the discipline he practiced. He thought of prayer not so much as a simple communication as a never-ending relationship. It was not so much a verbal exchange as it was an integral pattern of spiritual power coming to life in and through him.

When he worked with others to heal, redeem, and restore, he was aware of their spiritual endowment and sought to bring it to life through the mediating power of his faith. But his faith was not a foregone conclusion. He was always on trial in the maelstrom of life, and in this struggle for divine values he knew that he must always keep close to the source of his spiritual power through the life of perpetual prayer.

He never claimed that it was an easy discipline. In times of crisis when his need was great he struggled so strenuously that those who observed him said he sweated blood. But he believed with his whole being that God was on the side of his struggle for the spiritual meaning for life that could pervade and fulfill every human event with divine meaning. The cross with its mixture of suffering and triumph stands as the ultimate test and ultimate achievement of his faith-filled life.

When Jesus interpreted the life of prayer to his disciples by using the parables of the calloused judge and the grudging neighbor, he was not pointing out what God is like. Rather, he was making it clear that in our efforts to understand our relationship to God there must be an unending persistence. Jesus never asked anything for himself, but always that God's will might be realized in him.

Men may argue the fine points of the teaching of Jesus and in so doing may bring conflict and discord into the ranks of Christendom, but if they look at the quiet figure who went out alone to pray and returned with power of the spirit such as no other man has ever shown, they would not need to seek satisfaction in controversy. Rather they would find it in the answer to the question the disciples asked, "Lord, teach us to pray." They were the ones who had lived close to him. They had watched him in all of the circumstances of life. They saw his skills and his spiritually endowed humanity. They did not ask for the secret of his ability to speak with power in parables. They did not ask to understand his calmness in all manner of crises. They did not even ask for the main points of his theological system. They saw his life and they sensed the secret of his power. They asked the secret of his life of prayer for they knew it was prayer that had set him off from all the rest of humanity.

We can do nothing better to restore our faith to a place of power in our world than to ask the same question and seek diligently again the sources of his power.

40. FOCUS ON THE INFINITE

❦

I<small>F</small> prayer can make an important contribution to man's way of life, it can also become a significant source of that life of spiritual values we call eternal.

We live in a day when men try to deny or ignore their mortal natures. In a death-denying, death-defying culture we emphasize the values of youth, beauty, health, and vigor, as if there were something disloyal or inhuman about that accumulation of years that moves a man toward his death. Just because we tend to deny the physical reality of death, we are in a poor position to build a philosophy of life that is adequate for both life and death. The effort to escape the full meaning of the reality of physical death means that we are inclined to ignore also the responsibilities that are commensurate with our mortal natures. If we live only for the enjoyment of each today, and avoid its responsibilities, we may well fail to accept the important spiritual disciplines that best prepare us for today, tomorrow, and eternity.

Our faith has never run away from our mortality as far as our physical nature is concerned. We have recognized that man has a material body and a spiritual body. To nourish and care for one with disregard for the other is unwise. To live with such materialistic preoccupation that we ignore the spiritual nature is to revert to the levels of those beings who have not been endowed with a God-consciousness that is able to outlive the merely physical.

The spiritual concern cultivated through prayer reflects itself in three basic concepts. The first is the idea of the more than mortal, the immortal. This idea gives substance to the soul's invincible surmise that man is not made for death, for the dust. Yet our usual approach to immortality tends to be bound to the partial. Our materialism subtly affects our ideas of the immortal.

Those who think of life in merely biological terms tend to think of immortality as an extension of biology through propagation, as if to produce children were the answer to the quest for personal permanence. Those who think of immortality in social terms would give significance to the state or social institutions, as if the investment of the self in that which survives the self guaranteed their endless life. Those who think of immortality in religious terms seek to give permanence to the wishful thinking of the individual through institutionally supported promises. Others think of immortality as the philosophical presupposition developed to give emotional support to minds shaken by fear and insecurity. Those who think of immortality in psychological terms think of an aspect of the mind's life that persists beyond space and time. Those who would do research in psychic phenomena would justify the belief in immortality in the hope of finding some communication with a discarnate spirit, with the faint hope that one white crow is enough to prove that not all crows are black. Some would project a view of immortality on the basis of an educated surmise, believing that the fact that the idea is so prevalent in the minds of men must warrant the conclusion that such an idea has a basis in reality to establish its universality. Yet all such partial approaches to the immortality of man can only be incomplete, for they are based on a limited view of the nature of man. They fall short of the totality of meaning that is projected from the totality of being that is expressed through spiritual unity with the cosmic nature here and now which achieves a meaning for life that cannot be overwhelmed by the incident of death.

The second basic concept that must be explored to gain insight into the eternal nature of man's spiritual life is found in the analogy to metamorphosis. While it may be more common in nature than we realize, it is seen in its most familiar form in the life cycle of a moth. A creeping, crawling thing wraps itself up in a cocoon and appears to die. Cut open that cocoon and you will find only a formless mass of mush and goo. It appears to have no form and no life, to be completely disorganized. But there is a design and pattern at work even in the formlessness we observe. From the destruction of one form of existence another and more interesting form of life is being generated. In due time the cocoon bursts open and a thing of rare beauty emerges, to fly off as if it were accustomed to another realm of existence. It lays its eggs and starts another phase of the life cycle. From the formless a pattern was at work that transfigured and transformed the formless matter. While science can describe the process, it is baffled to explain all of the factors at work to produce new form from the formless. Meaning is found in great assumptions that may be described though they cannot easily be explained.

That the human can find a meaning for continued life beyond the return to physical formlessness calls for imagination and faith grounded in observation. Some of life is always beyond death's reach. At Johns Hopkins Medical School a culture of living tissue was taken from the body of a girl who had conquered a baffling disease. This culture continued to live years after the girl left the hospital. It has been used to save the lives of many stricken with the disease. It is flown to remote parts of the world on short notice. It will probably continue its saving work for many years to come. Is it hard to see the relevance of another life which fulfilled a saving mission at the spiritual level? Jesus said, "I am come that ye might have life that is eternal." Long after he ceased to live physically, the spiritual energy he produced which has been cultured by the church and its saints is used by men to extend the life of their spirits against the diseases of material preoccupation. The mission effort rushes this spiritual insight to those in need in distant places. The insight is alive with meaning that transfigures and transforms life.

A third idea has to do with the meaning of time. Time is so basic a concept that we cannot define it without using a synonym. But however we think of it, we sense that it is a convenience for the mind of man. Time may not be structural to the universe. We may be the only creatures isolated on an island of time in the midst of timelessness. The director of the British radiotelescope poses a question about sending men off into interstellar space. If a man returns to earth after a ten-year journey off into space there is no guarantee that his idea of time will be supported. He may find that he returns to a strangely different planet which has lived a thousand years in his absence. "A thousand years are as yesterday in thy sight." In the realm of eternal things time is irrelevant and unnecessary.

Put together the meanings of the three words Time, Metamorphosis, and Immortality, and a new idea emerges. The concern about how long we live becomes relatively insignificant, for how long gives way to how well. When life finds a meaning rooted in values mere extension in time becomes secondary. This brings a new meaning to the words of Jesus about abundant life. The treasure that is out of reach of moth and rust is the treasure stored in the realm of values that is beyond time, space, and material things. Eternal life is then not so much an extension in time as it is an extension of value.

Simone Weil reflects this concern for value when she writes, "The thought of death lends the colour of eternity to the events of life. If we were to be granted perpetual life here below, our earthly life would lose the eternity that shines through it." The mystic feeling of unity with the Creator and his creation always transcends the measurements that are employed with physical things and moves freely in the infinite and the timeless.

In our day, with spiritual values continually threatened by a concept of life measured by space and time, we see a new relevance for the disciplines of prayer that relate the whole being of man with the nature of God in the experience of unity that moves beyond materialistic standards of measurement. It may well be that this wise use of prayer may be essential to man's need to face the reality of physical death so that he can build a value structure that is adequate for both life and death. Unless a grain of wheat falls to the ground and dies, it cannot spring up into new life. The reality of physical death must be accepted honestly before the reality of the life of the spirit can be achieved. There is clearly a physical body, and there is a spiritual body. A preoccupation with the one may preclude proper consideration of the other. The discipline of prayer brings all of life under the influence of the spirit, and when its precedence is established, then it is that the things that occur at the physical plane are merely incidental to the things that give value and meaning to all there is.

The tragedy of little minds is that they limit life to little measurements. The wonder of great minds and spirits is that they are able to recognize the true height and depth and dimension of man's nature and live accordingly. The process of prayer that releases within man the power of his spiritual potential gives to life an actuality that no longer can be measured by a yardstick or a clock. It has already achieved the measurements of eternity. It is no longer a body with a soul, but is rather a soul which for a time inhabits a body, but is not bound by it. Rather it can be the instrument for discovering the life that springs eternal.

PART SEVEN

Conclusion

❦

CONCLUSION

❧§❧

WE have taken a long and careful look at prayer, its process, its relationship to the self, its discipline, techniques, and its fruits in life. All that we have said has relevance at the point where the individual employs his capacity for prayer to bring about a change in his life and its activities. This obliges us to face our failures, our willfulness, our basic rejection of the way of life for the ways of sin and death.

The essence of sin is separation from the God who would be at work within us. When Jesus was asked about that sin that could not be forgiven, he was quite explicit. There are no sins that cannot be forgiven except the sin of not wanting to know our need for a relationship with God that is the source of forgiveness. The sin of active and deliberate separation from God is the denial of our nature. When we cease to function within the bounds of the spirit with which we are endowed, we cease to bear the marks of spiritual beings. But even this condition need not be permanent, for the native endowment of man can always break through to assert itself and restore our freedom from denial and put us on the pathway toward fulfillment.

Sin can plague life with a great uneasiness. This uneasiness and the feeling of guilt can so preempt our thinking that we are unable to concentrate on God. So sin may be any type of action that acts as an escape from God. A person may so hypnotize himself with guilt feelings and the practices of escape that his mind is conditioned against his spiritual nature. Just as an injury to the mechanism of the eye may cause blindness, so the preoccupation with activities that obscure the relationship to God tends to blind the eyes of the spirit.

The chief task of the conscious mind is to know God and through that consciousness to flood all of the rest of being with a quality and attitude that change thought and action. When sin intervenes, it redirects the activity of the mind from its main task, and all of the rest of life suffers. Prayer is the mental activity that makes the deliberate effort to restore the conscious mind to its main function.

So it is that all prayer makes an important place for the act of confession and the search for forgiveness. Sin and guilt take away from life the blessings of free communication between creature and Creator. The act of prayer restores the relationship. Prayer becomes a form of healing action that restores life to right relationships, and from this new structure of being comes the unconscious conditioning that frees life from the attitudes that cause separation from God.

Prayer is an active agent in dealing with these causes of separation and denial at three different levels. The sins of the past that may tend to separate us from God through guilt and fear are relieved through confession and forgiveness. The sins of the present are limited by the strength to overcome temptation. The sins of the future are prevented by the replacing of poisoned intentions by improved motives, so that the future is not faced with fear, and the inclination toward revenge is modified by the process of healthy contemplation.

Prayer is also an active agent in helping a person to face reality. Life is destroyed by escape from reality. The important element in any approach to reality is a healthy confronting of one's self as he is. This calls for a stern discipline, but it is a prime requisite in facing God. We cannot face ultimate reality if we start from false premises. Beyond all of our defenses and subterfuges, beyond all of our sham and make-believe, there is the central and essential *me* who has to be faced.

To be able to stand in naked honesty before our Creator and measure what is being done with the part of creation that is entrusted to our care is a strenuous discipline, but it is essential if we would move beyond the separation of falsehood and truly contemplate the obligations of our selfhood.

We are cautioned "not to think of one's self more highly than we ought to think." But this is relative. Some persons with an unreasonable degree of low esteem may be in real need of thinking of themselves more highly in order to place the proper value upon what God has made. It may be important for their prayer life to establish a sound estimate of their own value in the sight of God and in their own eyes.

But there are those whose approach to life presumes more for their limited humanity than is warranted. While we would not condemn a healthy measure of self-esteem, we would point out the dangers of any unwillingness to see beyond the defenses we have set up to protect ourselves. What we are that makes us important is the endowment of God and not something for which we are primarily responsible. This relationship that makes us somebody of importance rests upon the ability to be humble enough to see our own limitations and operate within them.

At this point it is perhaps wise for us to try to understand what the saints have referred to as the annihilation of self. The term is not acceptable to our modern ears with our idea of the importance of the self. But some comparable concept must have a place in our thinking. We must learn the importance of eliminating the false ideas about the self as somebody before we can achieve the humility that becomes the basis for spiritual learning. The damage of false pride is not that it overdignifies man, but rather that it destroys the basis for any true dignity. When we assume a false sense of our importance, we endanger our concept of our finiteness and thus threaten that relationship that can be the basis for any true importance we can possess.

The kind of prayer that can help people see themselves as they are and maintain a proper relationship toward that which is the source of their being becomes the basis for helping them achieve what they can be.

Often prayer can be a healing agent for the troubled spirit by helping to restore clarity of vision. Many persons are busy fighting imaginary foes. Their suspicions master their living and they project their distrust into so much of life that they get little else in return. This encourages multiplication of feelings of insecurity and inadequacy that stimulate the very suspicions in the first place. These projections from the dim preconscious states within the being can be brought under the control of the conscious mind by the persistent practice of the prayer that keeps the experience and the relations of life in a clear picture and a proper perspective.

Unreasoned fears may supplant a healthy faith. The experience of life often generates the fears that make life a tragedy rather than a triumph. The ability to fill the mind with the riches of human experience that can restore faith and bring a balance to thinking is an important part of the process of changing people.

These various changes that can be wrought in the person who submits himself to the discipline of prayer are dependent upon the degree of diligence employed to become subject to that discipline. It is not an easy and trivial conditioning of the mind of which we speak. Rather, it is the stern directing of thought to the place where it becomes the conditioner of our living.

We have little enough practice in concentration. Our attention is continually being shattered by the claims of a noisy world that clamors for our senses. But the ability to bring thought to the vital center of life is, as the word "concentration" implied, a vigorous effort. But until God and his will become central in our living and thinking, we are not likely to be able to do much to effect a desirable change in our beings. The periphery of life must be kept in its proper place so that first things may be first. "Seek ye first the Kingdom of God and his righteousness, and all of these other things shall be added unto you."

This kind of prayer would move us beyond superficial judgments. It would be the instrument of self-discipline and would release the spiritual values that can help to make reality clear.

Prayer is a method for releasing the efficient self. This is not efficiency as generally evaluated by our culture. The self released is not the "go-getter self" but rather the "go-giver self." Life is enriched when we are able to bring the various selves under the dominance of the self that serves God's will and ultimate reality.

How easily we may be entrapped by trivial prayer! How often we find ourselves trying to bend reality to serve our small needs and desires! Such prayer starts from small premises and moves toward small ends. It may make the individual feel a sense of personal satisfaction, but it fails to achieve the grander context of life which is known when the self fulfills its nature in a supreme will. So prayer is not so much asking for the self as it is realizing the possibilities of the self. It is the art of learning to give, accept, and adjust rather than to get, reject, and dominate.

This kind of prayer marks the achievement of maturity within the structure of personality. How often persons think they are praying when they restate the childhood prayers that prepared them for a night's sleep in the early years of life. Such persons would be offended at a meal of pablum, but they feel content to nourish the most demanding and most rewarding relationship of life on a comparable diet. The prayer attitude we would achieve produces the finest fruits of maturity in the ability so to live and accept and adjust to others that understanding, sympathy, empathy, and cooperation become the keynotes of existence rather than its by-products.

In our quest for true spiritual maturity, let us start with ourselves, exert our best energy to discover the fullest revelation of our spiritual natures, and in so doing find our reunion with the God within who would express his nature through us in all of the thoughts, feelings, and acts of a dedicated life.

I.N.T. di God & ans. = unlimited forgiveness,
understanding & good will. p.119.